Chakapan Baba Panton
or
The Poetry of Baba Malay

Buku 7

Book 7 - The Poetry of Baba Malay

Chakapan Baba Ni Ari series

Baba Malay Today series

All Rights Reserved.
No part of this publication may be reproduced, stored in a retrieval system, or transmitted, in any form or by any means electronic, mechanical, photocopying, recording or otherwise, without the prior written permission of the publishers.

Theresa Fuller asserts the moral right to be identified as the author of this work.

Bare Bear Media

ISBN 978-1-925748-33-8 - Print

Cover by Helzkat Designs

Copyright October 2025©

Sincere thanks to my husband, Paul, who supported this work in every way possible. I love you.

Many thanks also to my proofreaders for their checking. Special mention to Tim Fuller, Rosalind Ang and Linda.

National Library of Australia
US Library of Congress

Published 3 November 2025

Introduction - Poetry

Language is powerful.

In writing this text, I applied the SHOW don't TELL method. I wanted the reader to be able to pick up this book and begin to learn. Much as you would pick up a game and play.

    Chobak.

    To try.

The Peranakans loved their language. And one way of showing that love was in the writing and speaking of panton. Or in some cases, battling (ber-balas) it out with panton!

I have always loved poetry hence, I did not think my Baba Malay Today series would be complete without dealing with the subject of poems or panton as they are known. Since starting this project I have learnt so much. I may go back to do further research as the topic was much bigger than I imagined.

I hope one day to be able to see panton competitions as in the days when the majority of the Peranakans were able to speak Baba Malay. This then is one of my aims as I come almost to the end of the Baba Malay Today series.

Don't worry if you can't write poetry. Just read and enjoy! And I hope a whole new world opens up to you.

This is Baba Malay; the language of the Peranakans.

YOUR language.

Baba Malay

Baba Malay is the language of my ancestors.

A language that I discovered late in 2021 was about to go extinct with fewer than a thousand speakers in the world. I took a course in Baba Malay taught by Kenneth Chan, author of *BABA MALAY FOR EVERYONE - A comprehensive guide to the Peranakan language*. This was my start to saving Baba Malay.

But I believed much more had to be done.

The book you hold in your hands is the result of my mad persistence to save my language. While there are books out there on Baba Malay, I found little in the way for children. As a teacher, I believe that to save a language we must start with the young.

I wanted a book that parents could give to their children.
One I could give to my kids.

This is my attempt.

Theresa, affectionately known in the Peranakan community as Bibek Theresa.

    Sydney,
    29th of May, 2022

Iau Kin

Iau Kin = Important

Contents

Introduction	3
Baba Malay	4
Contents	6
How to write a Panton	8
Rhythm	10
Rhyme	11
Types of Panton	12
Pantun Etymology	14
Pantun Possible Origins	15
Peranakan Background	26
Poems from Pantun Pilihan Peranakan Baba Negeri Selat	27
Note about the spelling	28
Budi	29
Puji-memuji	35
Pengajaran Nasihat	41
Sindiran Kiasan	47
Hajat Harapan	53
Gembira Hiburan	59
Janji Kecewa	65
Takdir Nasib	71
Rindu Dendam	77
Rasa Hati	83
Kebernaran	89
Kasih Sayang Cinta	95
Adat	101
Bermaaf-maafan	107
Sahabat Handai	113
Bertanya	119

Kuasa Tuhan	125
Amarah	131
Dagang	137
Perbandingan	143
Burong	149
Tumbuhan	155
Buah-buahan	161
Rencam	167
A Poet by any other name?	172
Why Panton?	178
Challenge 1	180
Challenge 2	182
Challenge 3	184
Challenge 4	186
Different Types of Peranakan Poetry	188
Syair	190
Dondang Sayang	191
Symbolism of Animals	193
Symbolism of Flowers	194
Symbolism of Plants	195
BONUS - Peranakan Penang Poetry!	196
My Poem	203
Dedication	207
Notes	208
About the Author	209
More books in the Baba Malay Today Series	210
Dear Reader	211
New Peranakan Tales Series	212
Other Books by the author	213
Presentations	214

How to write a Panton

Poem = Panton

Pantons are made up of 4 lines.

    Pembayang (foreshadowing) = First 2 lines
    Maksud (meaning) = Last 2 lines

Pembayang = generally sets the tone for the panton.

Maksud = provides the purpose of the panton.

The following panton was written by my Chikgu Kenneth Chan.

Burong trebang tinggi-tinggi,
Betol bebas betol bergangsi,
Senangkan badan, senangkan diri,
Itu-lah gua punya janji.

Translation:
Birds fly high in the sky,
Totally free having space to roam,
Taking life easy,
That is my destiny.

In the example shown on the previous page, we can see that the poem's first two lines (pembayang) are about birds flying freely.

The last two lines (maksud) explain the meaning of the poem. In this case the poet's aim, which is to lead a carefree life.

It is important in all panton that the meaning/message is clear.

NOTE: Pantun is standard Malay spelling.
Panton is Baba Malay spelling.
('Pantun' used when referring to pantun in general and 'panton' when referring to Peranakan poetry.)

Glossary

Bebas = Freedom
Bergangsi = From the word gansi meaning having freedom
Betol = True or correct
Burong = Bird
Gua = I
Itu = That
Itu-lah = That is it
Janji = Promise or Destiny
Punya/Mia = Ownership
Senang = Easy (Senangkan badan & Senangkan diri are two phrases that mean to take life easy)
Tinggi = High
Trebang/Terbang = Fly

Let's look at the rhythm next.

Rhythm

Poet = See Page 172

Aim for the rhythm or for the number of syllables to be between 8 and 10.

    2   2   2   2   = 8
Burong trebang tinggi-tinggi,

    2   2   2   3   = 9
Betol bebas betol bergangsi,

    3   2   3   2   = 10
Senangkan badan, senangkan diri,

    3   1   2   2   = 8
Itu-lah gua punya janji.

Rhyme

Burong trebang tinggi-tinggi,   **A**
Betol bebas betol bergangsi,   **B**
Senangkan badan, senangkan diri,   **A**
Itu-lah gua punya janji.   **B**

Here is an example by the late William Gwee:

Makan pais sama mengkudu   **A**   9
Makan sireh sama pinang   **B**   8
Bila terkenang tempu dulu   **A**   9
Ayer mata jatoh berlinang   **B**   9

Translation:
Eat some pais with cheese fruit,
Eat some sireh with betel nut,
When remembering days of past,
Tears fall in streams.

Glossary

Ayer mata = Tears (water eye)
Berlinang = Streams
Bila = When
Jatoh = Fall
Makan = Eat
Mengkudu = Cheese Fruit
Pais = A cake that resembles otak-otak
Pinang = Betel nut
Terkenang = Remembering

Types of Panton

A Word = Patah

A panton is a 4-line verse or poem. The following 8 types are taken from William Gwee's **a baba malay dictionary**:

Panton Budi = Theme gratitude

Panton Chetek = 4 line verses that are easy to understand

Panton Dagang = Theme sadness, loneliness (the word dagang actually means orphan or alien. Interestingly, it also means trade in Bahasa Melayu.)

Panton Dondang Sayang = Specifc genre that is sung (But to be honest, in the past all panton was sung.)

Panton Kaseh = Theme love

Panton Naseb = Theme destiny

Panton Rampay-rampay = Mixture of themes

Panton Sindiran = Theme innuendo

NOTE: The words above and their meanings have been taken from Gwee's dictionary.

When Editor Ding Choo Ming (**Pantun Pilihan Peranakan Baba Negeri Selat**) collected poems from the 1910-1930s, he came up with 24 divisions/types:

1. Budi = Theme of Kindness and Gratitude
2. Puji-memuji = Praise
3. Pengajaran dan nasihat = Teaching & Advice
4. Sindiran dan kiasan = Sarcasm and Figurative
5. Hajat dan harapan = Wish and Hope
6. Gembira dan hiburan = Happy & Entertainment
7. Janji dan kecewa =

Pantun Etymology

Pantun (Bahasa Melayu) = Panton (Chakapan Baba)

According to Bartosh, Kotova, Kytina and Kharlamova (Malay folk genre panton: traditions and modernity, 2023, Vol. 28 No. 1 61-78) "Pantun is a traditional genre of Malay poetry that traces its roots to medieval Malay folklore."

There are several theories as to pantun's etymology:

1) 'sepantun' - a Malay word that translates to 'like' or 'appropriate';
2) 'penuntun' - a Minangkabau word that translates to 'guide' or 'escort';
3) Merger of two words - 'pan' (polite or ethical) and 'tun' (leadership or mentoring);
4) 'parik' - Javanese word that is similar to the Malay 'pari' meaning peribahasa or proverb;
5) 'seloka' - Indian two-line verse form.

NOTE: Pantun is standard Malay spelling.
Panton is Baba Malay spelling.
('Pantun' used when referring to pantun in general and 'panton' when referring to Peranakan poetry.)

Pantun Possible Origins

There is a theory that the ancestors of pantuns were likely proverbs, aphorisms and two-line rhyming riddles. Thus, originally the pantun would have been simply a riddle used by the people to deceive the hostile spirits which is evidenced by the charms recited at that time.

Let's REWIND time:

Imagine a landscape filled with spirits.

In this world, almost everything had a soul: animal, mineral and vegetable. The soul of a man would appear as a thumbkin: "A thin unsubstantial human image," or "mannikin, temporarily absent from the body in sleep, trance, disease, and permanently absent after death." While the soul of an animal would appear as the animal itself, a tree's soul would take the shape of an animal, while ore such as gold would take the soul of a deer.

Divinities dwelt in this landscape. There was the 'White Divinity' who dwelt in the sun, the 'Black Divinity' who dwelt in the moon and the 'Yellow Divinity' who dwelt in the yellow sunset-glow (Sinjakala or twilight.)

To protect themselves from harm, charms such as these would be uttered:

(Following in Malay then English)

Mambang kuning, mambang k'labu,
Pantat kuning di-sembor abu.

Yellow spirit, grey spirit,
A yellow bottom sprinkled with ash.

The sayer would mock the spirit while spitting in his direction and throwing ashes. This was to extinguish the light so that the sayer would not contract a fever.

Pantuns were probably around in the pre-written era when poems were sung or performed with music. They were possibly concocted as a form of memory aid. These writers and performers were held in high regard. We see evidence of this in the prewritten literature, such as the tale of Bidasari and the Hikayat Pelanduk Jenaka i.e., the folktales of the mousedeer Sang Kancil also known as Akal Pelanduk and various other monikers.

The Syair Bidasari is a Malay ballad that tells the tale of the beautiful maiden Bidasari who falls into a deathlike sleep. In this epic, the first ballad is simply titled "Song 1" and tells the origins of the protagonist - Bidasari. See English translation opposite.

Basically, it is a romance entirely written in poetry which in the past used to be sung. This epic is also referred to as the Malay Snow White.

Once upon a time in the Malay world, there lived a girl whose beauty was so radiant it was said her life was tied to a magical fish. This is the story of Bidasari, a tale of love, envy, and survival that has echoed through centuries. When a jealous queen tries to destroy her, Bidasari's fate hangs in the balance.

And of course being a romance, the highlight is when the king meets the beautiful princess Bidasari.

(Malayan literature; comprising romantic tales, epic poetry and royal chronicles; by Bidasari; Shajrat malayu; Djouher-Manikam; Bukhari; of Johore, fl 1603; Starkweather, Chauncey Clark, 1851-1922; Marre, Aristide, 1823-1918; Devic, L. Marcel. Publication date: 1901)

BIDASARI

SONG 1

Hear now the song I sing about a king
Of Kembajat. A fakir has completed
The story, that a poem he may make.
There was a king, a sultan and he was
Handsome and wise and perfect in all ways,
Proud scion of a race of mighty kings.
He filled the land with merchants bringing wealth
And travellers. And from that day's report,
He was a prince most valourious and strong,
Who never vexing obstacles had met.
But ever is the morrow all unknown.
After the Sultan, all accomplished man,
Had married been a year, or little more,
He saw that very soon he'd have an heir.
At this his heart rejoiced, and he was glad
As though a mine of diamonds were his.
Some days the joy continued without clouds.
But soon there came the moment when the prince
Knew sorrow's blighting force, and had to yield
His country's capital. A savage bird,
Garouda called, a very frightful bird,
Soared in the air, and ravaged all the land.
It flew with wings and talons wide outstretched,
With cries to terrify the stoutest heart.
All people, great and small, were seized with dread,
And all the country feared and was oppressed,
And people ran now this way and now that.
The folk approached the King. He heard the noise
As of a fray, and angry, asked the guard,
"Whence comes this noise?" As soon as this he said...

English translation

Continued from Page 42 of Bidasari

Thy beauty is unspeakable; thou art
Above all crowns, the glory of all lands.
My soul adores thee. Lord am I no more
Of mine own heart. Without thee, love, I could
No longer live; thou art my very soul.
Has thou no pity to bestow on me?"
The more he looked the more he loved. He kissed
Her ruby lips, and sang this low **pantoum**:

Song

    Within a vase there stands a china rose;
        Go buy a box of betel, dearest one,
    I love the beauty that thine eyes disclose;
        Of my existence, dear, thou art the sun.

    Go buy a box of betel, dearest one.
        Adorned with *sountings* brave of sweet *campak,*
    Of my existence, dear, thou art the sun;
        Without thee, everything my life would lack.

    Adorned with *sountings* fair sweet *campak,*
        A carafe tall will hold the sherbet rare;
    Without thee, everything my heart would lack;
        Thou'rt like an angel come from heaven so fair.

    A carafe tall will hold the sherbet rare,
        Most excellent for woman's feeble frame.
    Thou'rt like an angel come from heaven so fair,
        Love's consolation, guardian of its flame.

At the approach of night the mantris said,
"What doth the King so long away from us?"
They were disturbed, the prince seemed so unlike
Himself and filled with such unrestfulness.
"I fear me much," then said a mantri there,
"That some mishap hath overwhelmed the King."

Now remember, this is a syair so the story is already in poetry. A syair is basically a long poem, not 4-lines.

So in this highly charged atmosphere when the king meets the princess, he does the only thing possible to declare his love. He breaks into even more poetry. Which is probably in his eyes, a more elegant or sophisticated form of poetry. This blatant example shows the high regard in which pantun is held.

Examing the syair, we can see evidence of international trade in the mention of 'tulips' plucked and Egyptian carpets.

Another epic - the Hikayat Pelanduk Jenaka - according to the late Professor Ian Proudfoot existed in written form as far back as Malay literature can be traced. 'The text's structures mimic oral story telling techniques at every level.' The story is highly episodic and cyclic, the stock phrase "brow and moustache and beard" being repeated, while at the same time, it is highly controlled.

*Setelah demikian maka pelanduk jenaka itu pun turunlah dari atas pusu itu; maka ia pergi kepada pohon ara, maka digorisnya dengan taringnya, keluar getah ara itu, maka disapukannya pada **keningnya dan misainya dan janggutnya**: lalu ia pergi kepada pohon lalang, maka **keningnya dan misainya dan janggutnya**...*

*After doing so, the tricky mousedeer descended from the anthill and went over to a fig tree. He scratched it with his fangs and the sap came out, and then he wiped it on his **brow and moustache and beard**. Then he went to a field of wild grass and wiped the heads of the grass on his **brow and moustache and beard**, turning white his **brow and moustache and beard**...*

(Proudfoot Ian. A "Chinese" Mousedeer Goes to Paris. In Archipel, volume 61, 2001. pp. 69-97; doi : https://doi.org/10.3406/arch.2001.3613. https://www.persee.fr/doc/arch_0044-8613_2001_num_61_1_3613)

In this prewritten era, the penglipur lara (soother of cares) were the story tellers. They spread folktales orally, often using rhythm, rhyme, imagery, and symbolism. These miniaturised tales overlapped with riddles, charms and proverbs, eventually becoming the pantun of today.

Pantun riddles were known as *teka-teki*. These were recited while travelling, at dusk which was the time when the power of the spirits was the strongest or near sacred places such as a *keramat* which is essentially the tomb or burial place of a holy person.

To understand how the pantun was used to thwart spirits we need to first understand the structure of the pantun which was basically divided into two parts:

beginning and ending.

The beginning is the allegory (pembayang, or sampiran). It features the area in which it was created e.g., toponyms, names of typical plants and animals, dialect words etc. Natural phenomena are used as specific metaphors. The first statement is often a metaphor for the second. The ending is the content (maksud or isi).

If the pantun is believed to have originated from riddles, then both parts of the riddle, the question and the answer are equally important.

This is an example of a riddle most would be familiar with:

Question: Why did the chicken cross the road?

Answer: To get to the other side.

Imagine what it would look like without the question:

Statement: The chicken crossed the road to get to the other side.

All the **fun** would be removed.

Here is a simple pantun (not tricking spirits):

> *Mushroom after mushroom is born;*
> *Rain drizzles day after day.*
> *We hatch like duck eggs,*
> *Thanks to the relentless care of the duck.*

Explanation: The first two lines infer that because of the rain the mushrooms sprout. The second two lines state that ducklings are hatched by a duck. Joining these lines together produces a gestalt i.e., because of a person's care, we thrive and grow.

In pantun, the first two lines describe the relationship between man and the universe i.e., they portray the macro world. The last two lines then portray the micro i.e., the wisdom that man has received from the universe.

But sometimes the pembayang and the maksud seem to clash.

> *One, two, three, six,*
> *Six plus one is seven.*
> *We planted a pomegranate with you.*
> *And the chestnut tree grew up to make everyone laugh.*

Explanation: The first two lines do not seem to be related. This strange contrast produces a comic result which is the aim of this pantun. So this mishmash is deliberate, and the people of that time would have known this.

Here is a pantun designed to thwart spirits:

> *Golden bananas carried on a voyage,*
> *One ripens upon a chest of wood;*
> *A debt of gold may be repaid,*
> *But a debt of kindness lasts till death.*

Explanation: The impossible fruit: confuses spirits with illogical imagery, while humans hear the moral of gratitude.

Here is one that most would be familiar with:

> *The mousedeer counts crocodiles in the river,*
> *One, two, up to a hundred more;*
> *When it ends, the count is never finished,*
> *What was numbered is lost in the flow.*

Explanation: Spirits trapped in infinite tasks; humans hear of the futility of greed.

Later, the solving of these riddles would be incorporated into important events such as weddings. Pantun also developed into the way the noble values of the elders could be passed on. Allegories helped soften the blow of any harsh criticism.

Penglipur lara known also as story tellers utilised panton in their work. These storytellers were present both at court and in the rural villages. Life was tough and it was a custom for the villagers to gather around the penglipur lara after a hard day in the fields and ease the cares of the day through the story telling.

The world in which pantun was formed was not simply the Malay universe, as trade influenced also the formation of words. There were the Arabs (remember the carpets from Egypt) as well as the Europeans (the tulips). Hinduism and other religions were also spreading.

By the time Chinese men sailed into Southeast Asia, they found that they were not alone. It is likely that their poetry may have also influenced the pantun. The following poem (paraphrased) is taken from a Chinese folktale - The Dragon King's Daughter, written by Li Chaowei circa AD 760-820.

Across the wide earth and grey skies,
Hear then the distant cries.
The fox thinks he is safe in his lair,
Yet a thunderbolt reaches him.
A man who is true and upholds right,
Returns my daughter to my sight.
Such service how can we repay?

Explanation: The first two lines suggest that against the immense sky, human suffering may appear insignificant. The fox is a symbol of cunning, who in his lair thinks himself safe, but heaven sees all. The next line shows that justice will prevail. Finally, the last two lines show that there has been a good resolution, with the speaker's daughter returned to the gratitude of the father.

Confucian belief may be seen in the action of the true man, while Taoist beliefs may be seen in the fox who is the symbol of a supernatural being in Chinese folklore. The thunderbolt may be heavenly justice.

Peranakan panton is believed to have been influenced by the Eastern 4-Act Structure called Qi Cheng Zhuan He which originated from China. Confirmed by Professor Ding Choo Ming.

In the past, pantuns were used as a duel of wits - berbalas pantun. The following example has been provided by Dr Soesilo:

(Note: I have not touched the spelling.)

Pantun (Teasing)

> *Buah mangga buah jambu*
> *Panen banyak untung seribu*
> *Anak siapa berbaju biru*
> *Kerjaannya main melulu.*
>
> *Mangoes ripe and guavas, too,*
> *Harvest brings a fortune new.*
> *Whose child in clothes of blue?*
> *Plays all day with naught to do!*

Balasan (Reply)

> *Pagi hari langitnya biru*
> *Mancing di laut dapat kerapu*
> *Boleh saja main melulu*
> *Asal pendidikan tetap nomor satu.*
>
> *Morning skies are clear and blue,*
> *Fishing trips bring grouper, too.*
> *Play all day if that you choose,*
> *Just let learning guide you through.*

Explanation: The first couplet/parallel sets the scene with imagery of harvest and gain, hence profit through hard work. This is contrasted against the idleness of the child in blue. Moral - children should use their time well.

Although the social expectations are set, the first pantun's tone is teasing.

The second pantun further softens the criticism, admitting that play is fine, so long as in the long run education is the focus.

Another example of pantun is the Dondang Sayang. See page 191.

I have tried to present the more popular examples. It is not the intention of this book to present every example.

If you wish to carry out your own research, examine these poems against the 3-Act Structure and the Eastern 4-Act Structure. Which do you think the poems were influenced by?

What about the circular structure? Is there any other structure that the poems could be compared to?

Find a book of poetry and try to do your own translation.

Finally, try composing your own poems.

Peranakan Background

Line = Kerat

When the Straits Settlements were formed in 1826, the Peranakans enjoyed many benefits. Under British rule, the Peranakans learnt Roman script in schools and began composing poems in Baba Malay although they were never formally taught the language at school. In the past Baba Malay was a spoken language. This makes it difficult to understand old Baba Malay today because of the many ways the words were spelt - words were added, replaced, changed, separated and even half-words created. Often only by examining the context can the actual meaning of the word be deciphered. But not always.

Some words are from Bahasa Melayu and sadly for some words their meaning is lost. In 1913, according to Shellabear "the language of the great Settlements and large towns and of the markets and shops everywhere, in fact the business language of the Malay Peninsula, is Baba Malay..."

(Page 51, W.G. Shellabear, Baba Malay, 1913)

With the coming of schools where the main medium of instruction was English, Baba Malay ended up being spoken only in the homes and by the women and children. They spoke the Alus (pure) register whilst the men spoke the Kasair (coarse) register.

Regardless, Ding Choo Ming states that what was important was that the Peranakans had sufficient vocabulary to be able to compose and in doing so express themselves, their views, their feelings and dare I say, their criticisms. In other words, what made the Peranakans Peranakan.

Poems from Pantun Pilihan Peranakan Baba Negeri Selat

This next section contains poems/panton from Pantun Pilihan Peranakan Baba Negeri Selat. For this, I am indebted to Nonya Ho Gaik Kim, a former lecturer at Seminari Theoloji Malaysia who helped by translating the old Baba Malay pantons into English.

I would also like to thank Jam Low for the many discussions we had while I birthed this book.

Thanks also to Kenneth Chan, my teacher for answering my questions.

And many, many thanks to Dr Daud Soesilo who despite an extremely busy schedule always found the time to respond to my questions.

Kam siah!

Note about the spelling

NOTE: The following poems are in old Baba Malay and in their original spelling.

This is to honour the intentions of the original poets and to maintain the poem's rhythm and sound. I felt that I would be doing a disservice to modernise the poems.

Similarly for all the poems provided by Dr Soesilo - the spelling is untouched.

The book will end with a modern poem of my own as my contribution to panton. Please note that I wrote the poem years ago.

It would be wonderful one day to be able to produce a whole book of poems in modern Baba Malay.

I hope these poems will inspire today's generation to rise up to the challenge.

Pantun is standard Malay spelling.
Panton is Baba Malay spelling.
('Pantun' used when referring to pantun in general and 'panton' when referring to Peranakan poetry.)

Budi

Good deeds and courtesy

Budi 1

A single word = Sepatah

    Bila kesebrang hujan pon rintek,
    Rintek habis basah bomi-nya,
    Bukan chantek sebarang chantek,
    Chantek dengan budi bahsa-nya.

Translation:

    When going across the rain pattered down,
    Drenching completely the ground,
    It is not any kind of beauty,
    But beauty with grace.

Notes

When I studied poetry in school, I was told that the translation of each poem was often very individualised. Feel free to agree or not.

Rain saturating the earth is an imagery for completeness. It is not just the surface but deep down. Hence this is beauty that is not skin deep but true beauty.

This poem and the others may be evidence of the Eastern 4-Act Structure but again more research is necessary.

Glossary

Basah = Wet
Bila = When
Bomi (Old Malay word) = Earth (Bahasa Melayu - Bumi)
    (Baba Malay - Tanah)
Budi = Qualities of mind
Budi Bahsa-nya = Manner, polite, civilised action, speech and behaviour (Bahasa Melayu)
Bukan = No or not
Chantek = Beautiful
Habis = Done/Finished (Baba Malay - Abis)
Kesebrang = Cross to the other side (Baba Malay - Seberang)
Pon = Also/Even (Baba Malay - Pun)
Punya/Mia/Nia/Nya = Belonging
Rintek = Drizzle (Baba Malay - Ujan rintek-rintek)
Sebarang = Thing (Baba Malay - Barang)

Budi 2

Book = Buku

    Anak itek pandai berlari,
    Anak angsa terlompat lompat,
    Rupa chantek senang di chari,
    Budi dan basa susa mendapat.

Translation:

    The duckling runs well,
    The cygnet jumps about,
    Good looks are easy to find,
    Good manners are hard to come by.

Notes

Birds are sometimes used in poetry because they are symbolic of one day leaving the nest as birds can fly. Ducks and geese are commonly raised in Malay communities. Usage of birds also relate to beauty. In this case the use of the baby duck and the cygnet could refer to poor and rich.

Here the poem contrasts external charm i.e., the antics of the two young birds in the first two lines with the final two lines which point out that true character is what is more important.

Feel free to agree or disagree.

Glossary

Anak = Child
Anak Itek = Duckling
Anak Angsa = Cygnet
Basa = Breeding or Manners (Baba Malay - Bahasa)
Berlari = Run
Chari = Find
Di = In
Pandai = Clever (Baba Malay - Panday)
Rupa = Appearance
Senang = Easy/To have free time
Susa = Hard (Baba Malay - Susah)
Terlompat-lompat = Jump or leap about

Puji-memuji

Praise

Puji-memuji 1

Poem = Panton

Anak itek anak angsa,
Terenang-renang di dalam kolam,
Kalau pandai menimbang rasa,
Di puji orang siang dan malam.

Translation:

The duckling and the cygnet,
Swimming in the pond,
A person who is considerate,
Will be praised day and night.

Notes

Birds appear to be often used in the teaching of good behaviour. The duck is still linked with the cygnet (poor and rich). The kolam or pond is seen as a home for animals. Here the young animals move together thus producing an imagery of harmony. The second parallel explains that people who are courteous, i.e., drawing from the example, are truly to be admired.

An interesting snippet is that both ducks and geese swim not just during the day but also at night.

Someone who has been raised well will always be a credit to their parents.

Feel free to agree or disagree.

Glossary

Dalam = In
Kalau = If (Baba Malay - Kalu)
Kolam = Pool/Pond
Chantek = Beautiful
Malam = Night
Menimbang = Weigh (Baba Malay - Timbang)
Memuji = Praise (Bahasa Melayu)
Orang = Human Being/Person/People
Puji = Praise
Rasa = Taste/Feel/Sensation
Siang = Early
Terenang-renang = Swimming (Baba Malay - Berenang-renang)

Puji-memuji 2

Monkey = Monyet

Anak Berok di tepi pantai,
Masok ka-bendang makan padi,
Biar burok kain di pakai,
Asal pandai mngambik hati.

Translation:

A baby ape by the beach,
Goes to feed at the paddy field,
Knowing how to win people's heart,
Is more important than clothing.

Notes

Monkeys can be seen foraging near rice fields and are often used to pick coconuts. They also perform tricks. This is an image that would have been very ordinary in the past.

Budi - virtue is highly valued. This is a reminder not to judge by appearance. This might be an example of winning people's hearts through warmth and kindness.

Feel free to agree or disagree.

Glossary

Anak Berok = Baby coconut monkey
Asal = Source (Baba Malay - Asair)
Bendang = Rice Field
Biar = Let (Baba Malay - Biair)
Burok = Ugly
Di = In
Hati = Liver (Technically the meaning is the liver, but in this context it means the heart.)
Kain = Clothing
Makan = Eat
Masok = To enter
Mngambik = Take possession (Baba Malay - Amek)
Padi = Unhusked rice grain
Pandai = Clever (Baba Malay - Panday)
Pantai = Beach (Baba Malay - Pantay)
Tepi = Edge/Brink

Pengajaran Nasihat

Teaching and Advice

Pengajaran (Baba Malay Ajairan) Nasihat (Baba Malay ?) 1

Needle = Jarom

Kalu ada jarom pata,
Simpan jangan dalam peti,
Kalu ada silap sa-pata,
Simpan jangan di dalam hati.

Translation:

If there is a broken needle,
Do not keep it in a box,
If there is a word wrongly spoken,
Do not keep it in the heart.

Notes

I keep coming across this poem so believe it is still popular.

This poem advises against holding grudges, giving the example of not storing a broken needle because it is useless and may accidentally injure someone.

Words that have hurt should be cast aside because the only person they are hurting are the ones who continue to hold onto them.

Feel free to agree or disagree.

Glossary

Ada = To have
Dalam = Inside
Hati = Heart (in this instance the heart is inferred)
Jangan = Don't
Jarom = Needle
Kalu = If
Nasihat = Advice (Bahasa Melayu)
Pata = Broken (Baba Malay - Patah)
Pengajaran = Teaching (Baba Malay - Ajairan)
Peti = Chest/Coffin
Silap = Technique/Know how (Baba Malay - Kilap)
Simpan = Keep

Pengajaran Nasihat 2

Porridge = Bubor

Masak nasik menjadi bubor,
Bubor berchampon dengan nila,
Hati susa baik di hibor,
Kalu tidak menjadi gila.

Translation:

The rice has turned to porridge,
The porridge is mixed with indigo,
A sad heart must be comforted,
Otherwise, one becomes insane.

Notes

When padi or uncooked rice becomes porridge is basically a saying that what is done is done and cannot be undone. Still in usage.

Indigo was used for medicinal purposes in the past but not today. It was also used in dyeing traditional fabrics like batik. Adding indigo to the porridge makes the deed even more irreversible.

Malay idiom: "Kerana nila setitik, rosak susu sebelanga" or "Because of a drop of indigo, the whole pot of milk is spoilt."

So basically, let it go or throw it out. Unconsolable grief may lead to a mental breakdown.

Feel free to agree or disagree.

Glossary

Baik = Good
Berchampon = Mixed up (Baba Malay - Champor)
Bubor = Porridge
Dengan = With
Gila = Mad
Hibor = Solace
Masak = Cook
Menjadi = To come into existence (Baba Malay - Jadi)
Nasik = Rice
Nila = Indigo Dye (In the past, there was belief that eating indigo could cure infections such as diptheria and the flu. Note: indigo plants may be toxic so do not try.)
Susa = Difficult/Sorrow (Baba Malay - Susah)
Tidak = Not (Baba Malay - Tak)

Sindiran Kiasan

Satire and Metaphor

Sindiran Kiasan (Baba Malay ?) 1

Rice = Nasik

    Niat sa-pingan nasik kunyit,
    Habis sembahyang bawak pulang,
    Bila dengar guntor di langit,
    Ayer tempayan habis di buang.

Translation:

    Make a vow with a plate of yellow rice (to the spirits),
    After prayer bring it home,
    On hearing the thunder,
    Water in the jar is emptied completely.

Notes

Rice is important to the Peranakans. Nasik Kunyet, also known as Nasi Kuning to the Malays and Indonesians has an auspicious meaning and is often served on special occasions. The colour yellow symbolises wealth. The dish is served in the hope of receiving health and prosperity in the new year.

The following is an excerpt from EATING THE LIVER OF THE EARTH:
"Thunder - As the east coast of Sumatra, the Malay peninsula and the West Coast of Borneo do not have active volcanos, the loudest natural sound was thunder. In this animistic culture, the belief was that thunder was the sound of God and that the thunder god was capable of *baliw* (punitive storms)."

Here someone is praying or worshipping simply with the intention of personal gain. So when they hear the thunder, they tip out water (small but guaranteed) even before the rain (bigger but not guaranteed) arrives.

Glossary
Ayer = Water
Bawak = Bring
Bila = When
Buang = Throw away
Dengar = Hear (Baba Malay - Dengair)
Guntor = Thunder of the Voice of Heaven
Kiasan = Metaphor (Bahasa Melayu)
Langit = Heaven (Baba Malay - Kayangan)
Nasik Kunyit = Saffron Rice (Baba Malay - Nasik Kunyet)
Niat = Aspiration/Intention
Pulang = Return
Sembahyang = Divine Worship (Baba Malay - Semayang)
Sa-pingan = One plate (Baba Malay - Satu Pinggan)
Sindiran = Satire or Innuendo
Tempayan = Earthern water jar

Sindiran Kiasan 2

Coral = Karang

Inchek Ali pergi ka Tanjong,
Singga ka barat mengantek karang,
Sudah habis padi sa-karong,
Tidak dapat burong terbang.

Translation:

Mr Ali went to the Cape,
Stop by in the west to pick coral,
A sack of padi is finished,
Not a single flying bird is caught.

Notes

In Malay culture, the name Ali means high or elevated. It may also be used to represent the 'everyman.'

Names may reflect at the very least that the Peranakans lived in a multicultural society that is aware of trade with other countries.

Ali heads for the cape but stops to pick coral. This long journey implies a lot of activity. He gets distracted with picking coral. The effort of snaring birds is unsuccesful even with a lot of effort and resources.

Feel free to agree or disagree.

Glossary

Barat = West
Burong = Bird
Dapat = Get
Inche/Inchek = Mister
Ka = Near (Baba Malay - Kat)
Karang = Coral
Karong = Sack
Mengantek = Guessing this is Collect/Take (Baba Malay - Amek)
Pergi = Go (Baba Malay - Pi)
Sindiran = Innuendo or satire
Singga = To break a journey at a place (Baba Malay - Singgah)
Tanjong = Cape (Bahasa Melayu)
Terbang = Fly

Hajat Harapan

Wishes and Hope

Hajat (Baba Malay ?) Harapan 1

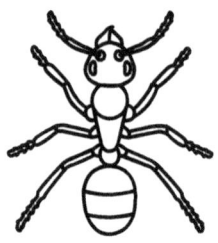

Ant = Semut

Tetak buloh panjang sa-puloh,
Handak di jolok sarang penyangat,
Angkat tangan jari sa-puloh,
Dokwa di mintak smua selamat.

Translation:

Cut the bamboo ten segments long,
To bring down the nest of stinging insects,
Raised hands with ten fingers clasped,
Praying that everyone will be safe.

Notes

You try to bring down a nest of stinging insects and pray no-one is injured.

The image of cutting bamboo appears to be a metaphor for human vulnerability. The ants are a symbol of danger. Peranakans appear to be superstitious.

Glossary

Angkat = Lift or carry
Buloh = Bamboo (Baba Malay - Bambu)
Dokwa = Prayer (Baba Malay - Semayang)
Handak = Want to (Baba Malay - Mo)
Harapan = Hope, trust, expectation
Jari = Fingers
Jolok = Poke
Mintak = Ask
Panjang = Length
Sa-puloh = Ten (Baba Malay - Sepuloh)
Sarang = Nest
Selamat = Safety/Peace
Smua = All (Baba Malay - Semua)
Penyangat = Stung (Baba Malay - Sengat)
Tangan = Hand
Tetak = Hack

Hajat Harapan 2

Star = Bintang

Bintan timor bergulong-gulong,
Chayanya sampay ditepi hutan,
Mintak umor setinggi gunong,
Mintakkan jerki bagi lautan.

Translation:

The eastern star twinkles,
Its light reaches to the side of the forest,
Pray for life as high as the mountains,
Pray for good fortune as wide as the ocean.

Notes

The Peranakans were brave to journey far in the quest for a better life.

Stars appear to be symbolic of luck.
Bintang dia gelap = Bad luck or misfortune.
Bintang dia terang = Good luck or fortune.

Or Bintang Timor might refer to the sun for afterall, the sun is a star and it rises in the east. Another clue that it might be the sun is the fact that the light of this star actually reaches to the edge of the forest.

The metaphors of the mountain and the ocean represent nature's grandeur and prayers for good fortune.

Feel free to agree or disagree.

Glossary

Bagi = Like
Bintan = Star (Baba Malay - Bintang)
Bergulong-gulong = Roll (Baba Malay - Gulong)
Chaya = Glow
Gunong = Mountain
Hutan = Jungle (Baba Malay - Utan)
Jerki = Fortune (Baba Malay - Jereki)
Lautan = The Sea or Ocean (Baba Malay - Laotan)
Sampay = To reach
Tepi = Edge
Timor = East
Tinggi = High
Umor = Age

Gembira Hiburan

Happiness and Comfort

Gembira (Baba Malay Hoa Hi and Hiborkan) Hiburan 1

Calf = Anak Kerbo

Anak kerbo mati tertambat,
Tinggi tinggi mata hari,
Niat berkaol sudah dapat,
Siapa tidak suka di hati.

Translation:

A calf that was tethered died,
High up in the sky is the sun,
A vow has been fulfilled,
Whose heart will not be happy?

Notes

The calf's death is symbolic of a sacrifice. Tinggi tinggi mata hari may refer to noon. Or the sun. This may mean that the sacrifice was blessed or witnessed.

This is the message - a vow fulfilled.

The last sentence is rhetorical: Who wouldn't be happy? (The question mark has been added by me.)

Si Matahari - Si is often a casual or familiar way of referring to someone or something. In this case, it is personifying the sun.

Feel free to agree or disagree.

Glossary

Anak Kerbo = Calf
Berkaol = Say a vow or promise
Dapat = To get
Gembira = Happy (Baba Malay - Hoa Hi)
Hari = Day (Baba Malay - Ari)
Hiburan = Entertainment (Baba Malay - Hiborkan Hati)
Tertambat = Tied. Often associated with the act of slaughter.
Mata = Eye
Mata Hari = Sun or Eye of the Day (Baba Malay - Mata-ari)
Mati = Die
Niat = Aspiration
Siapa = Who (Baba Malay - Sapa)
Sudah = Agreed (Baba Malay - Sua)
Suka = Like

Gembira (Baba Malay Hoa Hi and Hiborkan) Hiburan 2

Drum = Tambor

Tepok gendang tepok rebana,
Gesek biola ber-goyang kaki,
Kalu tuan bijak laksana,
Chobak kita berpanton lagi.

Translation:

Beat the gendang beat the rebana,
Play the violin shake the legs,
If you are smart and wise,
Let us do the responsive *panton* again.

Notes

Bergoyang kaki (shaking feet) generally refers to dance.

This is a simple panton. Basically, it means that if you enjoy dancing to this song or panton then let's berpanton (make panton) again.

Pantons were often sung to the accompaniment of drums and other musical instruments. This pantun reflects how panton was recited in social gatherings and the excitement of the berbalas pantun (responsive panton exchange.) You had to be wise and smart to participate.

Glossary

Tepok = To hit with the flat of the hand
Ber-goyang = Sway/Shake (Baba Malay - Bergoyang)
Berpanton = Chanting
Bijak = Talkative
Bijak Laksana = Used together to mean 'good at doing something.'
Biola = Violin
Chobak = Try
Gendang = Drum
Gesek = Swipe (Bahasa Melayu)
Kaki = Leg/Foot
Kita = We/Us
Lagi = More (Baba Malay - Lagik)
Laksana = As
Rebana = Small hand drum
Tuan = Master/Boss

Janji Kecewa

Promise and Disappointment

Janji Kecewa (Baba Malay Hanchor) 1

Bones = Tulang

Orang Hindi dari Singora,
Pergi ka Arab ka-lapan petang,
Tulang sendi tidak bergrak,
Jerki di harap bila kan datang.

Translation:

A Hindi from Singora,
Went to Arabia at eight in the evening,
Bones and joints are not moving (no work),
When will the good fortune hoped for come.

Notes

Portrays the extent to which a person may have to journey to find work. For a Hindu to travel to the land of the Muslims, things must have been dire.

Singora may be a place in Thailand but it is uncertain.

Travelling at unusual times may represent hardship as travelling at 8 at night seems a strange time. Or perhaps travelling in secrecy?

The lesson however appears to be that without effort hope remains unfulfilled.

Feel free to agree or disagree.

Glossary

Dari = From
Datang = Come
Bergrak = Move (Bahasa Melayu)
Harap = Hope/Trust
Kecewa = Disappointed (Baba Malay - Hanchor)
Lapan = Eight
Janji = Promise
Jerki = Luck (Baba Malay - Jereki)
Petang = Evening
Sendi = Joints (Bahasa Melayu)
Tidak = Not (Baba Malay - Tak)
Tulang = Bone

Janji Kecewa 2

Upstream = Ulu

Orang berkampong dari ulu,
Tanam kalapa berata rata,
Senang susa ku tanggong dulu,
Pada siapa mau berkata.

Translation:

People gathered from upstream,
Planted coconut all over,
Good or difficult times I bear them first,
To whom can I share them with.

Notes

Growing up in Singapore, we often used the term 'ulu' to describe a place that was far away or hard to reach.

The coconut is a member of the palm family and is found throughout Southeast Asia. It provides food, fuel, cosmetics, folk medicine etc. It has tremendous cultural and religious significance in certain societies and is often seen as a symbol of fertility and prosperity. The act of planting coconut trees symbolises family life. The planter had to sit cross-legged and close together as it was believed that this would cause the coconut to bear large and abundant fruit.

Thus it was common to find coconut growing near Malay homes. The first two lines suggest growth and togetherness contrasted with the last two lines which reflect loneliness despite wealth.

Feel free to agree or disagree.

Glossary

Berkampong = Village (Baba Malay - Kampong)
Berata rata = Level (Baba Malay - Rata)
Berkata = Said (Baba Malay - Kata)
Dulu = Before
Kalapa = Coconut (Baba Malay - Kelapa)
Ku = Me (Baba Malay - Gua)
Mau = Want (Baba Malay - Mo)
Pada = On (Baba Malay - Kat)
Senang = Easy
Susa = Difficult/Hard
Tanam = Bury in soil
Tanggong = To stand security
Ulu = Upriver

Takdir Nasib

Destiny and Fate

Takdir Nasib (Baba Malay Naseb)1

Ship = Kapair

Kapal di ulu dari sebrang,
Singga ke darat petek pala,
Diri siapa tak mau senang,
Suda tersurat di atas kapala.

Translation:

The ship upstream came from across the sea,
Stopped over to pick nutmeg,
Who does not want an easy life,
Destiny is already written on the forehead.

Notes

The Peranakans often tend to mention destiny. Tersurat means some thing obvious or directly stated in a text or expression. The ship's destination is unclear. However there is a famous place in Penang (Pulau Pinang) called Balik Pulau where one can drink nutmeg juice and purchase nutmeg souvenirs.

The word seberang may be the link to Penang as there are districts called Seberang Perai Utara(North), Seberang Perai Tengah(Middle) and Seberang Perai Selatan(South). And if you look at the map of Pinang, there is a district in the west called Barat Daya(Power). Or the word 'barat' may simply have been used to rhyme. Perai is a suburb of Penang. The word probably originates from Thai meaning 'the end.'

While people may desire wealth, everything is ulitmately in God's hands.

Glossary

Atas = Up/above (Baba Malay - Atair)
Barat = West
Darat = Dry land
Diri = Oneself
Kapala = Head (Baba Malay - Kepala)
Kapal = Ship or boat (Baba Malay - Kapair)
Mau = Want (Baba Malay - Mo)
Naseb = Destiny, lot in life, luck
Pala = Nutmeg (Baba Malay - Buah pala)
Petek = Pluck
Sebrang = Opposite side (Baba Malay - Seberang)
Singga = Break a journey (Baba Malay - Singgah)
Suda = Done/Finished (Baba Malay - Sua)
Takdir & Nasib = Destiny or Fate (Baba Malay - Naseb)
Tersurat = Something that is written (Baba Malay - Surat)
Ulu = High part of the river or upstream

Takdir Nasib 2

Letter = Surat

Inchek Kadok orang Jalotong,
Tanam mari ubi mengala,
Panday tak boleh malawan huntong,
Suratan sudah atas kapala.

Translation:

Encik Kadok is a man from Jalotong,
Come to plant potatoes,
Intelligence cannot fight luck,
Destiny is written on the forehead.

Notes

Inchek Kadok represents the common villager or the humble or naive man - See Pak Kadok the folktales. Using the name reinforces the theme of bad luck.

In the past, it was the norm for places in Asia to be named after the species of tree most common in an area. If Jalotong refers to the Jelutong tree then it is a species that grows in Malaysia, Borneo, Sumatra and southern Thailand. The jelutong tree can be tapped for latex and was a good source of timber. It was however overharvested in the past and is a protected species today. There are a few places in Malaysia named Jelutong - Melaka, Penang, and Johore. It could be Jelutong, east of Singapore in Johore. (Colless, Brian E. THE ANCIENT HISTORY OF SINGAPORE 1969).

Potatoes especially ubi keledek (sweet potato) were commonly eaten during the Japanese occupation becoming a staple to replace rice which was rationed by the Japanese.

The first two lines describe a common scene. The metaphor "written on the forehead" is an idiom that says that destiny is predetermined.

Glossary

Atas = Up/Top (Baba Malay - Atair)
Jalotong = Jelutong? (See above)
Kapala = Head (Baba Malay - Kepala)
Huntung = Make a profit (Baba Malay - Untong)
Malawan = Against/Opposite (Baba Malay - Lawan)
Mari = To come hither
Mengala = Take care (Baba Malay - Jaga)
Panday = Clever
Sudah = Finish (Baba Malay - Sua)
Suratan = Writing (Baba Malay - Surat)
Tanam = Bury in soil
Ubi = Tuber

Rindu Dendam

Deep Longing and Revenge

Rindu Dendam 1

Violin = Biola

Pergi di-tasek memanching haruan,
Champak jala kepala titi,
Bila ashek teringat-kan tuan,
Gesek biola hibor-kan hati.

Translation:

To the lake to fish snakehead fish,
Cast the net at the head of the bridge,
When I keep remembering you sir,
I play the violin to comfort my heart.

Notes

The first two lines employ imagery: a man casting a net as he fishes while the fish - ikan haruan - is commonly believed to assist in the healing of wounds.

And then there is the imagery of the violin, a popular instrument also used to bring comfort.

Glossary

Ashek = Fun (Bahasa Melayu - Asyik)
Biola = Violin
Champak = Throw down
Dendam = Revenge or hold a grudge
Gesek = Rub/Scrape
Jala – Net
Kapala titi = The edge of a pier
Haruan = Mud fish (Baba Malay - Ikan Aruan)
Hibor = Solace
Memanching = Fishing (Baba Malay - Panching)
Pergi = Go (Baba Malay - Pi)
Rindu = Passionate and sustained longing
Tasek = Lake
Teringat-kan = Remember (Baba Malay - Ingat)
Titi = Bridge
Tuan = Master/Boss/Lord

Rindu Dendam 2

Flower = Bunga

Inche Kachong orang di-pekan,
Gunting bunga beribu ribu,
Timbang berkabar terbang tinggi,
Tidak kuasa menanggong rindu.

Translation:

Mr Kachong is a man in town,
Cutting thousands of flowers,
Hearing the news feels distant,
I cannot bear the longing.

Notes

A poem about longing. Flowers symbolise affection or delicate matters of the heart.

Plants used in community life function as sources of food, beauty tools, medicine, therapeutic materials or in the use of rituals.

See chapter on symbolism of different flowers if you wish further information. Otherwise flowers are sometimes seen as symbolic of women because of their characteristics i.e., softness, beauty, fragrance and attractiveness.

The imagery of flowers by the thousands echoes the intensity of the pain of loneliness.

The name Kachong may simply be used for rhyming.

Glossary

Beribu ribu = Thousand (Baba Malay - Ribu)
Berkabar = News (Baba Malay - Khabair)
Bunga = Flower
Gunting = Scissors
Kuasa = Power
Menanggong = Stay (Baba Malay - Tinggair)
Pekan = Town (Baba Malay - Kota)
Rindu = Passionate longing
Terbang = Fly (Baba Malay - Trebang)
Timbang = Weighing
Tinggi = Lofty/Tall

Rasa Hati

Feelings of the Heart

Rasa Hati (Baba Malay Ati)1

Pepper = Lada

Orang berladang ditanah Acheh,
Chabot kopi tanam kan lada,
Bagi mana hati tak kaseh,
Apa kehandak semuanya ada.

Translation:

A man worked a plantation in Acheh,
Cleared the coffee trees and planted pepper,
How can the heart not be happy,
Whatever is desired is all here.

Notes

Acheh has been producing nutmeg since the 17th century. By 1820, it produced over half the world's supply of black pepper. In the early 19th century, Acheh's power increased due to its strategic location.

It is therefore assumed that its people must have been wealthy.

Replacing coffee with pepper suggests wisdom as pepper is more profitable. The last two lines portray emotional fulfillment, a consequence of wise decisions, hard work and contentment with what one has.

Glossary

Ada = To have
Apa = What
Bagi = Like
Berladang = Estate/Plantation (Baba Malay - Ladang)
Chabot = Flee/Pull out
Hati = Generally refers to the heart although hati literally means liver (Baba Malay - Ati)
Kaseh = Love
Kehandak = Want (Baba Malay - Mo)
Kopi = Coffee
Lada = Pepper
Mana = Where
Rasa = Sensation, taste, feeling
Semuanya = All (Baba Malay - Semua)
Tak = Not
Tanah = Land/Soil/Earth

Rasa Hati 2

Rice Field = Bendang

Padi di sawa rebah berdiri,
Di tanam anak pangkar rama,
Satu di Jawa kadua di Deli,
Tentu tak mau berjalan sama.

Translation:

The padi in the fields collapsed,
Planted by a person from the old jetty,
One is in Java and the other in Deli,
Definitely they don't want to walk together.

Notes

This was a difficult pantun to translate. Anak pangkar means bastard child, so did the second line mean the bastard child of Rama? The god Rama's wife had been kidnapped and Rama always suspected her of infidelity.

But there may also be another meaning. Anak means child and perhaps pangkar (archaic Malay?) means to plant carefully and so with rama meaning more (ramay?) it could possibly mean to 'plant more carefully.' Rama in Javanese also means father so perhaps this poem means the seedlings planted by the father/older farmer?

Just as the rice plants collapse, two people possibly lovers, are not fated to be together. This is shown by the distance. One is in Java and the other in Sumatra and they are separated by the sea. Jetties are places of departure so perhaps a parting is hinted at.

Glossary

Anak = Child
Anak Pangkar = Bastard Child
Berdiri = Stand up/standing
Berjalan = Walk (Baba Malay - Jalan)
Jawa = Java
Kadua = Second (Baba Malay - Kedua)
Mau = Want (Baba Malay - Mo)
Padi = Unhusked rice grain
Pangkar = ?
Rama = Father in old Javanese or Ramay as plentiful?
Rebah = Collapse
Sama = Same/Together
Satu = One
Sawa = Cultivated Land (Baba Malay - Sawah)
Tanam = To bury
Tentu = Certain

Kebenaran

Truth

Kebenaran (Baba Malay Betol)1

Poem = Panton

Kalu tuan turun ka-payah,
Betok lari aruan lari,
Kalu tuan kurang perchaya,
Kitab mari koran mari.

Translation:

If you go into the swamp,
The climbing perch runs away, the snakefish runs away,
If you don't believe,
Bring the Bible bring the koran (The purpose is for swearing.)

Notes

This poem is about trust. Like fish scattering when people approach, the truth may also be hard to come by when people doubt.

To swear on the holy book is to appeal to a higher authority. This was what was needed to rebuild trust in the past. Not common nowadays.

Glossary

Arun = Mud Fish (Baba Malay Ikan - Aruan)
Benair = Rational
Betok = Climbing perch (Baba Malay - Ikan Betok)
Betol = True
Kalu = If
Kitab = Scripture
Koran = Sacred book of Islam
Kurang = Less
Lari = To run/To flee
Mari = To come hither
Payah = Swamp/Morass (Baba Malay - Paya)
Perchaya = Believe; To have faith (Baba Malay - Berchaya)
Tuan = Master/Boss/Lord

Kebenaran 2

Bitter = Pait

Pegaga di potong-potong,
Kalau di urap tiada pait,
Orang meniaga mau kan untong,
Orang bersahabat mahu yang baik.

Translation:

Pennywort is cut into strips,
If made into a salad it is not bitter,
Those who trade want profit,
Those who make friends want good ones.

Notes

Pennywort is usually eaten raw as a salad (ulam) or used in drinks or snacks for its supposed health benefits.

Pennywort is bitter but can be made pleasant if prepared properly. Hence, like traders who seek profit, people want companions of good character.

Glossary

Baik = Good/Well
Bersahabat = Friendly (Baba Malay - Berkawan)
Mahu = Want (Baba Malay - Mo or mau)
Meniaga = Trade
Pait = Bitter
Pegaga = Pennywort (Baba Malay *unknown*)
Potong-potong = Cut/Slice
Tiada = None (Baba Malay - Tak ada)
Untong = Make a fortune
Urap = Food or cake surrounded by coconut
Yang = That/Which/Who

Kasih Sayang Cinta

Affection and Love

Kasih (Baba Malay Kaseh) Sayang Cinta (Baba Malay Kaseh) 1

Perau = Undecked ship

Prahu belayar pergi ka-Masay,
Angin sakal pata kamudi,
Hilang malu kerana kasay,
Hilang akal kerana budi.

Translation:

The boat sailed to Masir,
The wind came beating and the rudder broke,
Shame disappears because of love,
Reason disappears because of kindness.

Notes

Love is a powerful emotion. It can make people do silly things. The imagery of the rudder breaking shows the lost of control.

Besides love, deep gratitude may also cost loss of control. When you feel that you owe someone and need to repay that debt.

Glossary

Akal = Wit/Intelligence
Angin = Breeze/wind
Angin Sakal = Used together to mean strong winds/Headwind (the opposite of angin buritan)
Berlayar = Sailing (Baba Malay - Berlayair)
Budi = Qualities of mind and heart
Cinta = Love (Baba Malay - Kaseh)
Hilang = Lost (Baba Malay - Ilang)
Kamudi = After/Later (Baba Malay - Kemdian/Kemudian)
Kerana = Because (Baba Malay - Pasair)
Kasih = Love (Baba Malay - Kaseh/Sayang)
Malu = Shame
Pata = To break (Baba Malay - Patah)
Prahu = An undecked Malay ship (Baba Malay - Perau/Prau)
Sayang = Love

Kasih Sayang Cinta 2

Locheng = Bell

Orang Acheh pulang ka-kubu,
Bunyi locheng pukol lapan,
Jikalau dapat kasay setuju,
Sabagai pku lekat di-papan.

Translation:

The Achenese returned to the fort,
Rang the bell for eight o' clock,
When there is love and agreement,
It is like a nail stuck to a plank.

Notes

Bells are rung militarily for ceremonial purposes:

- marking the end of a watch;
- honouring departing officers;
- commemorating fallen soldiers.

Here the bell symbolises order with everything in place. And just like a bell ringing at the right time, if love is mutual then the relationship is off to a good start with a stable foundation. The relationshp can then be said to be as firm as a nail stuck to a plank.

Glossary

Bunyi = Sound
Jikalau = Kalu
Kasay = Love (Baba Malay - Kaseh)
Kubu = Fortification
Lapan = Eight
Lekat = Stick/Adhere (Baba Malay - Lengkat)
Locheng = Bell
Papan = Plank/Board
Pku = Nail (Baba Malay - Paku)
Pukol = Numerical coefficient for time
Pulang = To return
Setuju = Agree

Adat

Customs/Traditions

Adat 1

Pasair = Market

Pergi pasar manjual bli,
Orang China manimbang madat,
Budi basah tidak jual membli,
Idop dunia mau bradat.

Translation:

To the market to buy and sell,
A Chinese man weighs the opium,
Good manners are not bought and sold,
Living in the world requires custom.

Notes

Adat is the unwritten rules by which society is governed. But while goods can be bought and sold. kindness and virtue cannot.

The first two lines show normal trade although today we would not consider the buying and selling of opium to be legal among the populace.

The last two lines emphasise the importance of moral living which is intangible and not a commodity.

Feel free to agree or disagree.

Glossary

Adat = Custom or protocol
Basah – Manners (Baba Malay - Bahasa or Basa)
Bli = Buy (Baba Malay - Beli)
Bradat = Custom (Baba Malay - Adat)
Budi = Qualities of mind
Dunia = World
Idop = Being alive
Madat = Opium
Manimbang = Weigh (Baba Malay - Timbang)
Mau = Want (Baba Malay - Mo)
Manjual = Sell (Baba Malay - Juair)
Pasar = Market (Baba Malay - Pasair)

Adat 2

Gajah = Elephant

Anak gaja besar di hutan,
Di turut sakat anak kuda,
Orang raja saya bukan,
Di ikot pangkat mana yang suda.

Translation:

A baby elephant (calf) grew in the jungle,
Together with a family of foal,
I am not royalty,
Just follow the rank as in the past.

Notes

Pangkat equates to rank and is often a way to determine who leads and who follows.

This pantun teaches humility and acceptance of one's place in life.

An elephant in folktales often is a leader among the animals. A foal is considered a lesser ranked animal to the Malays. This is contrary to how the ancient Chinese viewed horses who were one of their most important animals.

Feel free to agree or disagree.

Glossary

Anak Gaja = Baby Elephant (Baba Malay - Anak Gajah)
Anak Kuda = Foal
Bukan = No/Not
Hutan = Jungle (Baba Malay - Utan)
Ikot = Follow
Orang raja = Royalty
Pangkat = Rank
Sakat = Supposed to be asalkan which means Provided (Baba Malay Asal - Origin)
Saya = I (Gua is used to express 'I' when the speaker is unfamiliar with the hearer and "Saya" when familiar)
Turut = Give way

Bermaaf-maafan

Forgiving one another

Bermaaf-maafan (Baba Malay Ampon) 1

Rusa = Deer

Rusa mati di dalam kebun,
Suda mati di jerat tali,
Dosa skali suda di ampon,
Suda ampon di buat lagi.

Translation:

The deer dies in the orchard,
Strangled by a rope,
The first wrong was already forgiven,
After being forgiven it is repeated.

Notes

One thing I learnt from an early age is that it is very hard to get a Peranakan to apologise. That's probably why the word 'maaf' doesn't exist in our dictionary.

Only in severe cases does a Peranakan apologise. Parents never apologise to their children.

A deer strangled in the orchard is an example of a person caught in their own actions. It is sad to see such a tragedy happen in a beautiful setting.

Meaning: someone who was forgiven has repeated the crime. This second mistake may not be so easily forgiven or forgotten.

Glossary

Ampon = To pardon
Bermaaf-maafan = Forgiving (Baba Malay - Ampon)
Buat = To do/Making
Dosa = Sin
Lagi = More (Baba Malay - Lagik)
Jerat = Noose
Kebun = Enclosed garden
Mati = Die/Death/Perish
Rusa = Deer
Skali = Times (Baba Malay - Kali)
Suda = Accomplished/Done with/Finished (Baba Malay - Sua)
Tali = Rope

Bermaaf-maafan 2

Kitab = Scripture

Bunga jalatang karang tak harom,
Kiriman anak Datok Penghulu,
Kitab terbentang bichara blom,
Mana patot di ampon dulu.

Translation:

The nettle is no longer fragrant later,
Sent by the son of the Village Chief,
The holy book is opened but without a trial,
Inappropriate to extend forgiveness first.

Notes

Every village had a headman, generally the oldest (and hopefully) the wisest man there. He was often called the Ketua/Tua or the Penghulu.

Nettle no longer fragrant carries little value. Hence forgiveness that is rushed is empty of meaning.

Glossary

Ampon = Pardon/Forgive
Bichara = Talk (Baba Malay - Kata)
Blom = Not Yet (Baba Malay - Belom)
Bunga = Flower
Datok = God/Deity
Harom = Nice scent (Baba Malay - Wangi)
Jalatang – Nettle (Bahasa Melayu - Jelatang)
    or it could be the Jelutong (Baba Malay) tree which is a large Rubber Tree)
Kiriman = Sent (Baba Malay - Kirim)
Kitab = Scripture
Kitab Terbentang = Used together to mean a Tome
Patot = Just/Proper/Fair
Penghulu = Headman (Baba Malay - Pengulu)
Terbentang = Open (Literally stretched out)
Tua = Old or in this case the Head of the village

Sahabat Handai

Friends

Sahabat Handai (Baba Malay Kawan Sedia) 1

Kelapa = Coconut

Klapa mudah dari Pringgit,
Buat mari makan serabat,
Biar hilang s'ribu ringgit,
Jangan ku hilang satu sahabat.

Translation:

Young coconuts from Pringgit,
Bring them to eat with relatives,
Let me lose a thousand ringgit,
Don't let me lose a single friend.

Notes

The coconut is a wonder fruit. It provides sustenance and is an essential ingredient in Southeast Asian cooking.

First two lines show a simple yet happy ocassion. This poem shows that friendship is more important than money.

Glossary

Biar/Biair = Let
Buat = To do/Making
Dari = From
Handai = Ready (Baba Malay - Sedia)
Hilang = Lost (Baba Malay - Ilang)
Jangan = Don't
Klapa = Coconut (Baba Malay - Kelapa)
Makan – Eat
Mari = To come hither
Mudah = Young (Baba Malay - Muda/Mundah)
S'ribu = A thousand (Baba Malay - Seribu)
Sahabat = Friend (Baba Malay - Kawan)
Sahabat Handai = It is unclear if this phrase refers to 'ready friends' or 'good friends.' Good friends = Kawan baik
Satu = One
Sedia = Ready
Serabat = Relatives (Baba Malay - Anak Beranak)

Sahabat Handai 2

Biola = Violin

Kalu gesek gesek biola,
Bolay gesek lagu bangsawan,
Chuma sedikit di amek mara,
Bila kan lama bolay berlawan.

Translation:

If playing the violin,
A bangsawan song can be played,
Taking offence over a very small matter,
How long can friendship last?

Notes

The violin was often one of the instruments used in making music when a panton was sung.

The first two lines portray harmony. Likewise relationships also require harmony. Hence being quick to take offence destroys harmony.

Glossary

Amek = To take possession
Bangsawan = Malay Opera
Biola = Violin
Bolay = Can (Baba Malay - Boleh)
Chuma = Only
Gesek = Rubbing past a fixed object
Lagu = Song
Lama = Length of time
Lawan = Fight
Mara = Angry (Baba Malay - Marah)
Sedekit = Little (Baba Malay - Sikit)

Bertanya

Asking

Bertanya (Baba Malay Tanya) 1

Keladi = Yam

Tarek tarek batang kladi,
Kalu kladi ada solor nya,
Ilang raip di sangka mati,
Jikalu mati mana kubor nya.

Translation:

Pulling the stem of the yam,
If it is a yam it has a tuber,
Vanished and thought to be dead,
If dead where is the grave?

Notes

Yams and sweet potatoes were often cooked in coconut milk.

Lots of possible meanings. Is this grieving for a lost someone? Or something metaphysical?

The poem appears to question assumptions: because someone is missing it does not necessarily mean that they are dead. In the case of Bidasari, she was thought to be dead but was really in a trance as the fish which contained her soul had been taken.

The Peranakans believed that the soul (semangat) was able to be detached. Thus the body was still alive although the soul was not attached.

Glossary

Ada = To have
Batang = Shaft/Stem
Bertanya = Ask (Baba Malay - Tanya)
Jikalu = If (Baba Malay - Kalu)
Kladi = Yam (Baba Malay - Keladi)
Kubor = Grave/Tomb
Punya/Mia/Nia/Nya = Belonging
Mana = Where
Mati = To die
Raib = To disappear
Sangka = Suspect
Solor = Rhizome or tuber of the taro (keladi) plant. Old Malay word.
 (Baba Malay - Ubi)

Bertanya 2

Buaya = Crocodile

Inchek Yayah orang Brunei,
Panday skali bermain jala,
Bukan ka buaya penunggu sungei,
Bangkay yang mana anyot ka kuala.

Translation:

Mr Yahya is a man from Brunei,
Very skilled at casting the net,
Is not the crocodile the guardian of the river,
What carcass drifts to the river mouth?

Notes

In folktales there are two main predators in the rainforest:
- crocodile
- tiger

Interestingly enough, they are both kings. The crocodile was the King of the River while the tiger was King of the Land. Crying crocodile tears was a common saying. It meant faking distress because crocodiles were rumoured to cry as they devoured their victims.

The first two lines set an everyday scene. A fisherman working hard. The second two lines show a failure of the crocodile as the King of the River, for a carcass has escaped him. In the past, the crocodile was seen as sacred.

Many possible meanings. Perhaps diligence is contrasted with accountability. Leaders who fail to fulfil their role.

Yahya is the Arabic form for John but it may be used here simply to suggest a skilled man who ironically cannot escape his fate.

Glossary

Anyot = Drift
Bangkay = Carcass/Corpse
Bermain = Play (Baba Malay - Main)
Buaya = Crocodile
Jala = Net
Kuala = Delta/River Mouth (Bahasa Melayu)
Panday = Clever
Skali = Times (Baba Malay - Kali)
Sungei = River
Penunggu = Wait (Baba Malay - Tunggu)

Kuasa Tuhan

The power of God

Kuasa Tuhan 1

Dewi = Minor divinity

Daywa daywa melaykat sakti,
Diam di dalam gua batu,
Maka ku tidak susa di hati,
Susa nya ada Allah membantu.

Translation:

Gods, goddesses, magical angels,
Dwell in the rock cave,
Therefore my heart is not sad or worried,
When in difficulty God is there to help.

Notes

I remember as a child being told by my grandmother to never water the garden in the evening as the fairies were sleeping.

And that a chicak would drop its tail into the ear of a child who told tales.

The spiritual was often intertwined with everyday life.

Here the panton is saying that even in difficult times, God is there.

Glossary

Allah = God (Found in the Baba Malay bible)
Batu = Stone/Rock
Dalam = Inside
Daywa = Demi-god (Baba Malay - Dewa)
Diam = Quiet/Still
Gua = Cave
Kuasa = Power or authority
Maka = Then (Baba Malay - Kemdian or Kemudian)
Melaykat = Angel (Bahasa Melayu - Malaikat; Baba Malay - Sian)
Membantu = Help (Baba Malay - Bantu or Tolong)
Sakti = Divinity

Kuasa Tuhan 2

Kuala (Bahasa Melayu) = Delta

Dari Kuala Berangin timor,
Turun sulatan balek pagi,
Di bri Allah itu lad umor,
Tak kan bolay terlebay lagi.

Translation:

From the east of Kuala Berangin,
Head south and arrive in the morning,
God determines our age,
It cannot be more than that?

Notes

The first two lines show a journey. This could symbolise the journey of life. This has a fixed starting and ending point. It could also represent the cyclical journey of life.

Similarly, the last two lines confirm that humans have a fixed lifespan determined by God.

Feel free to agree or disagree.

Glossary

Bolay = Can (Baba Malay - Boleh)
Bri = Bring (Baba Malay - Beri)
Kuala = The delta or wetland area that forms when a river empties into another body of body (Bahasa Melayu)
Lad – Length or duration Old Malay word (Baba Malay - Panjang)
Lagi = More (Baba Malay - Lagik)
Pagi = Morning
Sulatan = South (Baba Malay - Selatan)
Terlebay = More (Baba Malay - Lebih)
Timor = East
Turun = Descend
Umor = Age

Amarah

Anger

Amarah (Baba Malay Marah) 1

Ayam = Chicken

Ibu ayam dudok mengram,
Pecha menetas di-bawah dapor,
Slagi ku tidak lepas-kan gram,
Rasa sakit tulang di-tubor.

Translation:

The mother hen sits on her eggs,
They hatched under the stove,
As long as I don't let go of anger,
The bones in my body aches.

Notes

The chickens I remember while growing up were bantams. They were fierce!

When we were living in a flat we would place our scraps in a tin. Once a week the pig farmer would collect those scraps to feed his pigs. To thank us, he would give us a chicken each year.

The chickens were alive and it always fell to my mother to decapitate and pluck them.

The first two lines show a chicken brooding. This is analogous to a person brooding with anger. The message is to let anger go.

Glossary

Amarah = Anger (Baba Malay - Marah)
Ayam = Chicken/Fowl
Bawah = Below
Dapor = Kitchen
Gram = Anger (Baba Malay - Geram)
Ibu = Mother
Lepas = To free (Baba Malay - Lepair)
Mengram = Incubate (Bahasa Melayu - Mengaram)
Pecha = Break (Baba Malay - Pechah)
Pecha Menetas = Used together to mean hatch
Rasa = Feel/taste
Sakit = Sick (Baba Malay - Saket)
Slagi = So long as (Baba Malay - Selagi)
Tubor = Body (Bahasa Melayu - Tubuh, Baba Malay - Badan)
Tulang = Bone

Amarah (Baba Malay Marah) 2

Paya = Swamp

Kalau tuan pergi ka-Kedah,
Singga mandi dalam paya,
Brapa kwat brapa gagah,
Apa endah kepada sahya.

Translation:

If you go to Kedah,
Drop by to bathe in the swamp,
However strong or however brave,
What is that to me?

Notes

Many parts of coastal Malaysia were swampy. Kedah was swampy because of its low-lying coastal flood plan and poor natural drainage. Swamps could be seen either as a place of danger or of fertility. It is the liminal boundary between land and water and can be used either way in panton.

Animistic Malaysia was a land inhabited by spirits, so bathing in a swamp could be seen as something foolhardy. The water being murky could also be a metaphor for tangled politics. Swamps are breeding grounds for plants and animals like the sacred crocodile.

In ancient China a swamp would have been a tougher hunting ground.

Either way, the result is that whether or not you are brave, I am indifferent.

Glossary

Brapa = How much (Baba Malay - Berapa)
Endah = Care/Pay attention (Baba Malay - Sedairkan)
Gagah = Daring
Kepada = To (Bahasa Melayu)
Kwat = Strong (Baba Malay - Kuat)
Mandi = To bathe
Sahya = Me (Baba Malay - Saya/Gua)
Singga = Break a journey (Baba Malay - Singgah)
Tuan = Lord
Paya = Swamp
Pergi = Go (Baba Malay - Pi)

Dagang

Sadness & Loneliness or Trade

Dagang 1

Sauh = Anchor?

Pukol lapan pukol sembilan,
Bunyi tambor kuliling kota,
Suda dapat angin sulatan,
Angkat saoh blayar kita.

Translation:

Eight o'clock nine o'clock,
The sound of the drum across the city,
The south wind is here,
Weigh the anchor and we sail away.

Notes

Ships had to wait for the tide before sailing.

Drums often signalled the marking of time.

The first two lines show a sense of everything being ordered.

The last two lines continue on this example with the wind providing the right timing or opportunity to set sail or act.

Feel free to agree or disagree.

Glossary

Angkat = To lift
Angin = Wind
Blayar = Sailing (Baba Malay - Berlayair)
Bunyi = Sound
Dagang = Trade in Standard Malay (Baba Malay - Meniaga)
Dagang = Orphan, Alien, Foreign hence sadness (Gwee's dictionary)
Going through the poems both trade and sadness are present.
Perhaps because merchants/traders struggle so much to survive.

Kota = City
Kuliling = Surroundings (Baba Malay - Keliling)
Lapan = Eight
Saoh = Anchor Sauh (Baba Malay - Sauh in the Baba Malay bible)
Sembilan = Nine (Baba Malay - Semilan)
Suda = Finish (Baba Malay - Sua)
Sulatan = South (Baba Malay - Selatan)
Tambor = Drum

Dagang 2

Nakhoda (Bahasa Melayu) = Captain

Datang lanchang nakoda besok,
Meniaga dengan nakoda puri,
Bagaimana dagang nak masok,
Di timbang blom chukay negri.

Translation:

The ship of the captain arrives tomorrow,
To trade with the captain of the city,
How do traders want to come in,
When the state has not calculated the taxes.

Notes

Traders always preferred free ports to ports that charged taxes. This was why the British ports were always more popular.

The first two lines show opportunity with the ship coming in to trade. But the last two lines show that trade cannot happen if the state has not set proper regulations.

Feel free to agree or disagree.

Glossary

Bagaimana = How (Baba Malay - Amcham)
Besok = Tomorrow
Blom = Not yet (Baba Malay - Belom)
Chukay = Tax
Dagang = Trade or Traders
Dengan = With (Baba Malay - Sama)
Lanchang = Type of sailing ship used as a warship, lighter and as a royal ship.
Masok = Enter
Meniaga = Trade
Nak = Want (Baba Malay - Mo)
Nakoda = Skipper (Bahasa Melayu - Nakhoda)
Negri = Country (Baba Malay - Negeri)
Puri = Temple or Shrine
Timbang = Weigh

Perbandingan

Comparison

Perbandingan (Baba Malay Banding)1

Silat = Traditional Malay martial arts

Budak-budak main senjata,
Bersilat-silat tengah padang,
Brapa trang api plita,
Mana-kan sama sinaran bintang.

Translation:

Little kids playing with toy weapons,
Doing the silat on the field,
No matter how bright the light of a lamp,
It can never be as bright as a shining star.

Notes

Similar to today, in the past many practised martial arts.

Like children imitating real warriors; the light of a lamp cannot outshine the light of the sun.

Both are feeble imitations of something far greater. Our creations cannot match God's creations.

Feel free to agree or disagree.

Glossary

Api = Fire
Banding = Ponder (page 33 of the dictionary)
Bersilat = Traditional Malay Martial Arts (Baba Malay - Silat)
Bintang = Star
Budak = Child, Budak-Budak (Children)
Brapa = How much (Baba Malay - Berapa)
Main = Play
Padang = Field
Perbandingan = Comparison (Baba Malay see Banding above)
Plita = Lamp (Baba Malay - Pelita)
Sama = Same
Senjata = Weapon
Sinaran = Star Shine/Rays/Light
Tengah = Middle
Trang = Bright (Baba Malay - Terang)

Perbandingan 2

Kain = Cloth

Deri kandang ka-Kampong Srani,
Anak China menjual kain,
Ibarat bachang dengan kweni,
Rupa-nya sama rasa lain.

Translation:

From kandang to the Eurasian village,
A Chinese sells cloth,
Like salom fruit and saipan mango,
They look the same but taste different.

Notes

A Kandang was an enclosure for animals such as water buffalo. These enjoyed wallowing in the mud and thus tended to turn the ground into a muddy quagmire.

The first two lines simply show an everyday scene. But at the same time, the liminal mention of the 'Srani' or Serani meaning Eurasian reinforces the theme of something that is familiar and yet foreign, paralleled with the fruit which looks the same but is different.

Things may appear outwardly the same but are very different on the inside.

Feel free to agree or disagree.

Glossary

Anak China = Chinese
Bachang = Horse Mango (Baba Malay - Buah Bachang)
Dengan = With (Baba Malay - Sama)
Deri = From (Baba Malay - Dari)
Ibarat = Like (Baba Malay - Sama)
Lain = Different
Kampong = Village
Kain = Cloth
Kandang = Fenced enclosure
Kweni = Might be a type of sour mango (Baba Malay - Kueni)
Menjual = Sell (Baba Malay - Juair)
Rasa = Taste
Rupa = Appearance
Srani = Eurasian (Baba Malay - Serani)

Burong

Birds

Burong 1

Burong = Bird

    Amek tempurong di bakar bakar,
    Isi mari di dalam dulangi,
    Laksana burong di dalam sangkar,
    Kalu tak mati tentu terbang.

Translation:

    Take the coconut shells and burn them,
    Put the kernel in a tray,
    Like a bird in a cage,
    If it is not dead it will surely fly away.

Notes

Chinese love their birds. I remember coming across men sitting around, surrounded by birds in cages singing.

I always felt sorry for the birds as they were big and the cages small.

Again a domestic scene showing the preparation of coconuts. What is useful is retained.

Captivity is temporary - the bird will escape or die.

Basically saying that nothing lasts forever.

Feel free to agree or disagree.

Glossary

Amek = To take possession
Bakar = To burn
Burong = Bird
Dulangi = Tray (Baba Malay - Dulang)
Isi = Flesh or Fill up
Laksana = Like (Baba Malay - Sama)
            Normally used in idioms
Mati = Die
Tempurong = Half of a coconut shell used as a ladle
Terbang/Trebang = Fly
Tentu = Certainly
Sangkar = Cage

Burong 2

Sangkar = Cage

Tetak kayu di pagi hari,
Hendak di buat tiang bumbong,
Sunggu bijak si burong nori,
Lebeh bijak si burong tiong.

Translation:

Chopping wood in the morning,
Want to make a pillar for the roof,
The parrot is really smart,
Much smarter than the mynah.

Notes

I remember watching as a man fed his bird. To do this, he picked up small brown crickets, broke off their hind legs and then slid them into a slot on the side of the bird cage.

I was horrified.

First two lines show ordinary events. Pillars are symbolic of strength and support.

Last two lines praise the more intelligent parrot, thus showing that people always gravitate to the more capable.

Feel free to agree or disagree.

Glossary

Bijak = Talkative
Bumbong = Main beam of the house
Burong Nori = Parrot (Baba Malay - Burong Kakaktua)
Burong Tiong = Myna/Mynah, also known as the Indian myna
Hari = Day (Baba Malay - Ari)
Kayu = Wood
Lebeh = More
Pagi = Morning
Tetak = To hack

Tumbuhan

Plants

Tumbuhan (Baba Malay Tumboh) 1

Bunga Siantan = Ixora Flower

Dimana ruma Chek Tipa,
Di balek ruma asam kumbang,
Bagaimana hati tak suka,
Bunga kunchup balek kembang.

Translation:

Where is Cik Tipa's house?
Behind it is the asam kumbang tree,
How can the heart not be happy?
A flower bud is fully bloomed upon my return.

Notes

Chek or cik is a Malay honorific for a young woman. Tipa is probably the short form of Fatimah or Siti and the two words portray an image of an ordinary Malay girl of marriageable age.

Mangos were always a favourite of the Peranakans and so they tended to grow them beside their houses. Asam kumbang though is supposedly an uncommon fruit. It can be eaten with sambal belacan or pickled.

First two lines show an everyday scene.

Last two lines bring the message of returning home to find that love has blossomed.

Feel free to agree or disagree.

Glossary

Asam = Sour/Tamarind
Asam Kumbang = Mangifera quadifida - a type of mango tree (Bahasa Melayu)
Bagaimana = How (Baba Malay - Amcham)
Balek = Going back
Bunga = Flower
Chek = Mr/Uncle (Baba Malay - Inche/Inchek or Che)
Kembang = Expand/Swell up
Kumbang = Beetle
Kunchup = Kiss (Bahasa Melayu - Kucup)
Ruma = House (Baba Malay - Rumah)
Tumbuhan = Plants (Baba Malay - Tumboh)

Tumbuhan 2

Bunga Raya = Hibiscus

Abang Ali menjual tapay,
Lagi Malaka ka bukit baru,
Brapa wangi si bunga rampay,
Bunga di pokok terlebay bau.

Translation:

Ali's older brother sells tapai,
From Malacca to Bukit Baru,
No matter how fragrant the potpourri,
The flower on the plant is more fragrant.

Notes

This ending is something I agree with. I have always preferred to leave flowers on the plant rather than pick them.

First two lines show an everyday scene of buying and selling. To me, a real flower is always more beautiful than an artificial flower.

Tapai is a delicacy made from glutinous rice (pulut) and often eaten on special occasions. Bunga Rampay is often prepared for special occasions as it gives off a fragrance that is welcome by all.

In the past Bukit Baru may have been considered a separate place but today Bukit Baru is part of Malacca.

Feel free to agree or disagree.

Glossary

Abang = Big brother (Baba Malay - Hia)
Bau = Scent/Odour
Baru = New
Brapa = How much (Baba Malay - Berapa)
Bunga Rampay = Potpurri of shredded leaves and flower petals
Bukit = Hill (Baba Malay - Buket)
Lagi = More (Baba Malay - Lagik)
Malaka = Malacca
Menjual = Sell (Baba Malay - Juair)
Tapay = Fermented pulot rice (Baba Malay - Tapai)
Terlebay Bau = More smell so more fragant (Baba Malay - Terlebeh bau)
Wangi = Fragrant

Buah-buahan

Fruits

Buah-buahan 1

Arimo = Tiger

Rimau ini resmi betina,
Mati di sempang amek anaknya,
Laymo ini laymo China,
Setaon sekali nampak buahnya.

Translation:

The tiger shows characteristics of a female,
It died at the junction and its cub was taken,
These oranges are Chinese oranges,
Once a year the fruit will be seen.

Notes

It is a tradition when visiting to not come empty handed. I remember my mother choosing mandarins. One for each hand.

I wonder if this is why Peranakans call gifts buah tangan.

The first two lines depict a tragic story - a tigress dying and her young being taken.

Oranges in the past appear for a short time once a year. So value what is rare. Similarly, life is short as shown by the sad story of the tigress.

Feel free to agree or disagree.

Glossary

Betina = Female (Baba Malay - Prompuan)
Buah = Fruit
Buah-buahan = Fruits
Ini = This
Laymo = Orange (Baba Malay - Lemo manis)
Lemo = Lime
Manis = Sweet
Mati = Die
Nampak = To be visible/To see
Resmi = Officially (Bahasa Melayu)
Rimau = Tiger (Baba Malay - Arimo)
Sempang = Branching off
Setaon = One Year (Baba Malay - satu/sau taon)

Buah-buahan 2

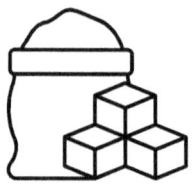

Gula = Sugar

Ini gula masak di Malaka,
Masak di tapis dari dusun,
Dari mula saya tak sangka,
Nampak manis menjadi rachun.

Translation:

This sugar is cooked in Malacca,
Cooked and filtered at the orchard,
From the beginning I didn't suspect,
What looks sweet became poisonous.

Notes

I love Gula Melaka and all its desserts.

The traditional method is to extract the sap from the bud of the coconut flower. The sap is then boiled down.

In this poem, we see that appearances can be deceiving. Malacca was renown for its trade which included sugar.

Sugar could possibly be symbolic for charm and beauty. While poison could be symbolic for pain and betrayal.

Possibly a love poem portraying betrayal.

Feel free to agree or disagree.

Glossary

Dusun = Village (Baba Malay - Kampong)
Gula = Sugar
Masak = Cook
Manis = Sweet
Menjadi = Become (Baba Malay - Jadi)
Mula = (Baba Malay - Mulai)
Nampak = To see
Rachun = Poison
Sangka = Suspect
Tapis = Filter

Rencam

Mixture of different types of panton

Rencam (Baba Malay Champor) 1

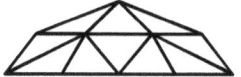

Intan = Diamond

Ikan duri Kuala Johor,
Kail orang di Tanjong Surat,
Intan berduri suda mesohor,
Nampak rengan di timbang berat.

Translation:

The catfish from Kuala Johor,
Caught by a person in Tanjung Surat,
Precious stones are well known,
Looks light but heavy when weighed.

Notes

Rosecut diamonds are characterised by a flat base and a dome shaped top with a small number of facets (3 to 24).

The first two lines appear to simply provide rhythm. Or else symbolism that is unknown. Is this referring to someone who is difficult, like a thorny fish?

When one fishes, it is not clear if one will catch anything.

Don't judge a book by its cover.

Feel free to agree or disagree.

Glossary

Berat = Heavy
Duri = Thorn
Ikan = Fish
Intan = Rose cut diamond
Intan berduri = Diamond with thorns
Kail = Hook (Baba Malay *unknown*)
Kuala = Delta (Baba Malay *unknown*)
Mesohor = Popular (Baba Malay - Mashohor)
Rencam = Mix (Baba Malay - Champor)
Rengang = Light not heavy (Baba Malay - Ringan)
Suda = Finish (Baba Malay - Sua)
Timbang = Weigh
Tanjong = Cape (Baba Malay *unknown*)

Rencam 2

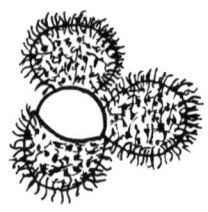

Rambutan = Rambutan

Rambutan di pukol ribot,
Abis gugor akan bunganya,
Intan manikam apa di sebot,
Bukan ka temaga besar gunanya.

Translation:

The rambutan tree was lashed by the storm,
All its flowers fell,
Why talk about precious stones,
Is not brass of great use.

Notes

Rambutans are another favourite to bring as a gift when visiting.

One bunch is sufficient.

A rambutan tree was lashed by the storm, thereby stripping it of its flowers. This is symbolic of fragility.

Jewels are admired but in reality it is the common metals that are more practical.

Feel free to agree or disagree.

Glossary

Abis = Finished
Akan = Will (Baba Malay - Mo)
Besar = Big
Bukan = No/Not
Bunga = Flowers
Intan = Rose cut diamond
Gugor = To drop prematurely
Guna = To use
Manikam = Precious gemstone (Baba Malay Berharga - Valued,
    Baba Malay *unknown* = Gemstone)
Nya = Its
Pukol = To strike or beat
Rambutan = Fruit (Rambut - Hair, by adding the 'an', it becomes hairy fruit.
Ribot = Storm/Strong Wind
Sebot = Utterance (Baba Malay - Sebut)
Temaga = Copper or Brass

A Poet by any other name?

Poet = ?

A problem I encountered soon after starting this project was the mystery of what the Baba Malay equivalent word was for the writer of pantons i.e., poet. I had assumed it would have been a simple matter of asking the experts or at least looking up the dictionary, but to my surprise, almost a year later I was still on the search for that elusive goal.

Just what did the Peranakans call their poets?

Here are some possibilities:

1. Penyair - This is apparently the standard Bahasa Melayu title of a 'poet' and one that Malay speakers would be familiar with. However, syair are not panton;

2. Orang Sajak - This translates to 'person of poems' with the word 'sajak' being the modern translation of poem. The problem with this definition however is that the sajak(poem) is not panton as sajak are free verse and conversational;

3. Poet - In Singapore, the rule is generally to use an English word if its Baba Malay equivalent cannot be found;

4. Orang Karang Panton - Translates to mean 'person who composes panton';

Interestingly, when our Peranakan ancestors selected words, there was a method. I refer to BABA MALAY by W.G. Shellabear, 1913.

Page 55 - Words of household affairs, religious ceremonies, business affairs, medicine and games have been borrowed from the Chinese language.

So what would be the possible term for poet in Hokkien?

(Hokkien is mainly comprised of Tsuan-tsiu Hokkien (Central and Southern Malaysian) and Tsiang-tsiu Hokkien (Northern Malaysia and Kuching) with Singaporean Hokkien skewing towards Tsuan-tsiu Hokkien.)

詩人 (*si-jîn* or *si-lîn* in POJ Romanization)

Breakdown:

詩 (**si**) = poem / poetry

人 (**jîn / lîn**) = person (in Hokkien not Mandarin)

So 詩人 literally means "poetry person" — i.e., a **poet**. (Literary reading).

Was this the answer to my question?

I looked to the Peranakans in Penang to see if they had an answer.

Like the Peranakans in Singapore and Malacca, the Peranakans in Penang also originally spoke Baba Malay. However they were flooded by refugees from China in the early part of the 20th century due to the many wars on mainland China. This is why today Peranakans in Penang speak Hokkien instead of Baba Malay.

I looked up the Penang Hokkien-English Dictionary by Tan Siew Imm and this is what I found:

Poet = Si-Ong

Poem = Si

The Peranakans in Penang, according to Lim Hiong Seng A MANUAL OF THE MALAY COLLOQUIAL 1887, stated that the Malay in Penang differed from that of Singapore and Malacca. In fact they speak Hokkien but they do still use Malay words.

According to Tan Chee-Beng, the Babas were pioneers among the Chinese to publish in Malay. A number of them published panton and syair in book form. 'The Baba interest in Malay poems and music represented dynamic Baba involvement in Malay cultural activities. In the process, they also created Malay poems in Baba Malay.'

Baba Malay today still holds a large number of words which are Hokkien in origin.

But what was the answer to my question?

I turned to the Bible translators in the end.

I contacted Dr Daud Soesilo. Dr Soesilo was born in Indonesia and completed his D. Min at Vanderbilt University and Ph.D in OT studies at Union Presbyterian Seminary. He has served with the United Bible Societies for 37 years full-time and enjoys working with the Malayo Polynesian language family - the indigenous languages of Taiwan to the Tokelau in New Zealand, the Malagasy of Madagascar to the Maori of the Cook Islands, the Suriname Javanese in the Dutch Guyana, plus Malay and Baba Malay.

When I asked him what the word for poet was in Baba Malay, his answer was pujangga.

I was relieved as finally I had my answer.

But then as I was finishing off this book, I came across the research of Bartosh, Kotova, Kytina and Kharlamova (Malay folk genre pantun: traditions and modernity). From them I learnt that the writers of pantun are called pemantun.

This was later confirmed in the 2016 lecture by Professor Dr Ding Choo Ming to Baba House who referred to poets as pemantun.

As poem in Baba Malay is spelt panton and not pantun, I believe the spelling should be pemanton.

So I am pleased to be able to say that in Baba Malay a poet is either:

- pujangga; or
- pemanton

Take your pick!

Chobak
To try

Why Panton?

I love poetry but I am not a poet.

So a series of textbooks would just not be complete without an introduction to panton. And this is a snippet to hopefully whet your appetite. But because I am not a poet, I have only concentrated on panton and not syairs or the dondang sayang.

I encountered a lot of difficulty in bringing this book to life.

The first problem was sourcing poetry. I am indebted to the many who have gone before me and provided the groundwork. These Baba Nonya according to Ding Choo Ming (The Malaysian Baba Pantun Database, *Sari 22 (2004) 159 - 165*) developed a body of literature using Romanised Malay by the end of the 1890s.

Although I have been taught to write panton by my chekgu Ken Chan, it was only one lesson and we wrote a single poem each. Hence, I depended on the expertise of others for assistance. Kam siah!

From Dr Soesilo who grew up with pantons, I learnt that pantons are still a part of everyday life in Indonesia. Domestic flights end announcements with the recitation of pantons. "They are a means of special communication within communities that blend wit and the beauty of artistic expression. Often in a gathering a pantun by one group will be responded by another pantun from another group."

In Iban Malay, pantun means 'song' so the Anglican Hymnbook is called Surat Pantun. The second problem I had was in the understanding of the pembayang and the maksud. This is how Dr Soesilo explained the pembayang: "The connections between the first two lines and the last two lines vary from one pantun to another. Sometimes it is the sound, sometimes the rhymes, sometimes the lexical connections (mind you, these features are difficult to translate, or even untranslatable into English.) Hence, you can't fully appreciate the beauty through translation alone... "

According to Jimmy Khoo Seng Kiong, "The word 'Pantun' describes a type of poem recited to a set rhythm against a musical background of a Malay folk tune. Not so many years ago it was common practice among the Baba society to indulge in this form of entertainment... The art of 'selling' a poem by the singer and the immediate response by yet another singer 'buying' in his or her rebuttal with the appropriate reply will always create an atmosphere of joy in any gathering."

Panton used to be sung to the accompaniment of a violin, rebanas and a gong.

According to Raymond Kwok MALAY ECHOES FROM THE PAST, PENANG HOKKIEN - BABA LANGUAGE, 'Such rendition of love poems or "pantuns" was a flute and an accordion with tambourines to keep the tempo.'

For a challenge, the following pages contain poems selected from MALACCA POEMS published by the Persatuan Peranakan Cina Melaka in memory of the late Baba Lee Chee Lin. There are four themes: Kaseh, Budi, Puji-pujian and Sindiran. Try your hand at translating them.

Dr Soesilo's other projects include the Vietnamese Study Bible, the Hmong Bible, Cooks Islands Maori Bible, the Ajie OT of New Caledonia, the Tongan OT, Persian Bible Revision Project, as well as being a guest professor at various international universities.

Challenge 1

Poet = Pemanton

Sribu burong trebang,
Mari hinggap di sawa padi,
Bila rindu ulang ulang,
Bau sedap di dalam hati.

Translation:

Thousands of birds fly,
Coming to perch on the cultivated padifields,
...
...

Explanation

Start by compiling a glossary of the words. What words can you find in Baba Malay? What words are in Bahasa Melayu? Can you find the equivalent Baba Malay word?

Once you have translated as many words as possible, read the poem over a few times.

What do you think the poet is trying to convey?

Sadly, although a few books on poetry exist, the poems very seldom contained an English translation.

Glossary

Bila =
Burong =

Challenge 2

Poet = Pujangga

Amek hutan menebang kayu,
Amek papaya sa-bijit lada,
Budi tuan banyak telalu,
Budi saya mana yang ada.

Translation:

Explanation

Start by compiling a glossary of the words. What words can you find in Baba Malay? What words are in Bahasa Melayu? Can you find the equivalent Baba Malay word?

What do you think the poet is trying to convey?

Glossary

Amek =
Budi =

Challenge 3

Cup = Changkir

Orang tua dudok berchakap,
Amek changkay tuang ayer,
Suka hati tak bolay chakap,
Sbagai itek berjumpa ayer.

Translation:

Explanation for yourself

Glossary

Amek =
Budi =

Challenge 4

Tiger = Arimo

Nampak bulat di sangka lemo,
Sayang sa-bijit di paytak kangkong,
Tuan pakay kulit arimo,
Hendak gretak rusa sa kampong.

Translation:

Explanation for yourself

Glossary

Bulat =
Kulit =

Different Types of Peranakan Poetry

The pantun, syair and the dondang sayang are different types of Malay poetry according to Ding Choo Ming (2004). Each has its own distinctive structure, style, rhyme and formula. Ding also suggests a different origin - folk poetry.

The Chinese that initially came to the Straits Settlements were the poorest of the poor, but many eventually prospered as they skilfully adapted to the local environment i.e., learnt English. Ironically, it is also this skilful adaptation that is responsible for the decline of Baba Malay today.

Clammer (Clammer, John R. 1979. The Ambiguity of Identity: Ethnicity Maintenance and Change Among the Straits Chinese Community of Malaysia and Singapore:ISEAS) claims that "Baba culture is a rare and beautiful blend of the dominant elements of the Malaysian and Singaporean cultural traditions... a genuine synthesis..."

Ding Choo Ming confirms that the Peranakans' poems were coloured by Chinese folktales and characters and that these poems were extremely popular with reprintings every two years. Through these poems the Peranakans described their life, experiences and visions. The pantuns are 'still marvelled at for their ingenuity and creativity' and 'among the most highly valued pieces of literary work'.

Ding concludes with his hypothesis:

'1. Many baba authors recreated old expressions that they remembered,
2. They tended to make use of earlier material, or bits of Malay pantun,

3. Standardised formulas were grouped around standardized themes,
4. A group of words is regularly employed under the same metrical conditions to express a given essential idea;
5. Formulaic thought and expression were deeply imprinted in them,
6. Tradition and innovation were complementary forces, which to gether assure meaningful communication,
7. They combined earlier materials by following the style, structure, rhythm and language norms of the pantun, syair or dondang sayang,
8. The audience for Baba's literature was essentially a mixed one - Babas, Chinese and Malays - which made it natural for the authors to combine multi-ethnic themes and methods.'

See www.atma.ukm.my for a pantun, syair and dondang sayang database for more poems.

Syair

Djikalaw belajar harapan angin
Itoe toewan tanah poenja kepingin,
Sijang dan malam boewat pikirin
Takoet keleboeh jang di selempangin

If it were a sailing-ship, they hoped for wind,
Such was the desire of the landowners;
Night and day lost in thought
Afraid lest the ship may sink.

Kreta api itoe selempang,
Orang ta'oesah toeroet menoempang,
Djalan lempeng tijada menjimpang,
Tijada chawatir denganja gampang.

With the train there's nothing to fear,
No need to accompany the freight,
The line is straight without deviating,
With the train there is no worry, it is east.

(Part of a Poem (Syair) by Tan Teng Kie 1890 - The Batavian Eastern Railway Co. and the Making of a new "Daerah".)

The syair is in some ways basically a longer version of the panton. Each stanza or quatrain consists of 4 lines which rhyme AAAA or BBBB or CCCC. The syair is normally 8-12 syllables per line and contains an ongoing story.

Although pantons may be linked, it is generally agreed that they are independent and that the final rhyme is abab. The final difference is that in the panton, there are two distinct halves: the maksud and the pembayang. Hence the syair is often simply a lengthy poem. There is no allusive quality unlike the panton. There is a lot of debate about the origins of the word syair which has numerous spellings.

Dondang Sayang

According to the Gunong Sayang (Mountain of Love) Association in Singapore, dondang sayang is 'a form of poetry singing' done in public. Also known as 'musical debating' where two or more singers compose and exchange pantons in an impromptu fashion.

Dondang Sayang parties were the norm at Peranakan events such as weddings, birthdays and deaths.

As is well documented, by the early 20th century many Peranakan familes including my own decided to have their children educated in English. Thus began the decline of Baba Malay as a ubiquitous language spoken by the Peranakan man in the street.

Many of the pantons in this book were sung as Dondang Sayang. Here is an example provided by Dr Soesilo:

(Note: the spelling is untouched.)

Gran tenglam tepi daratan
Berisi pasir dengan batu
Baru smalam ku mimpi tuan,
Sbagi kasay ada di pangku.

A sunken rock lies by the shore
Filled with sand and stones once more
Just last night I dreamed of you,
As if my love was in my arms true.

Explanation: The first couplet is filled with imagery of nature. The last two lines turn inward with the expression of a dream in which the lover was held.

Reply

>Seray mati lengkuas mati,
>Tanam mari Pulau Panjang.
>Cheray mati puas di hati,
>Cheray idop mata mer-mandang.
>
>Lemongrass dies, galangal dies,
>Planted over on Pulau Panjang.
>If the face is gone, the heart is satisfied,
>If the face lives, the eyes keep gazing.

Explanation: The first two lines foreshadow bad news with the plants. The location may or may not have another meaning. The final two lines show the extent to which emotion is expressed - contentment if the face is absent and fixation if present.

The dondang sayang is a duet. One singer starts off with a metaphor of fate and sweet love and the following singer concludes with loyalty and commitment.

Symbolism of Animals

Anjing (Dog) = Bad luck, possibly murder (MM)
Arimo (Tiger) = Symbol of Strength (FT)
Ayam (Chicken) = Intelligent but coward (FT)
Babi (Pig) = Humiliation (FT)
Eagle = Strength, symbolises powerful people (FT)
Gagak (Crow) = Bad luck, great calamity (MM), linked with humans with a bad attitude (FT)
Gajah (Elephant) = Good luck (MM), Power (FT)
Kaldei (Ass) = Bad luck (MM)
Lembu (Draught cow) = Good luck (MM)
Musang (Fox) = Evil. Symbol of male predator (FT)
Naga (Dragon) = Safe from stumbling blocks (MM), Strength (FT)
Nocturnal birds = Ill-omened (MM)
Peacock = Beauty and arrogance (FT)
Sapi (Dairy Cow) = Bad luck (MM)
Semut (Ant) = Industry (FT)
Singa (Lion) = Good luck and prosperity (MM), Strength (FT)
Sparrow = Commoner (FT)
Swan = Commoner who likes to travel but remembers its roots (FT)
Tiong (Magpie) = Goodness (FT)

NOTE: MM = Denotes that the source reference is Malay Magic
FT = Denotes that the source reference is Folk Tales.

Often no symbolism is used and the animal simply represents itself.

Symbolism of Flowers

There is a standard symbolism that flowers usually represent women while bees or beetles represent men. At all times the context must be considered.

Rose (Bunga Mawair) = Therapeutic, Fragrant, Beautifying

Cambodia (Bunga Kamboja or Frangipani) = Fragrant, Medicinal, Beautifying, Therapeutic. (Interestingly grown in cemeteries)

Flower Kenanga (Cananga odorata) = Fragrant, Ritual (wedding, remembrance of ancestors and in witchraft)

Fragrant flowers tend to be used in flower bath therapy.

Basil Flower = Food

Jasmine (Bunga Melor or Jasminum Sambac) = Beautifying, Fragrant, Medicinal (sinusitis, fatigue, headaches, increase breast milk), Ritual (weddings and death). Jasmine symbolises purity and loyalty because of its clean white colour.

Bunga Senduduk (Melastoma Malabathricum) = Medicinal (Child birth and staunching wounds, diarrhoea, removal of smallpox scars, Haemorrhoids and Toothache).

Symbolism of Flowers and Plants source is FUNGSI BUNGA-BUNGAAN DALAM TEKS PANTUN MELAYU 'BINGKISAN PERMATA' by Azyantee Mohd Zawawi, Nurmasitah Mat Hassan, Nordiana Ab Jabar 2022.

Symbolism of Plants

Padi = Commonly associated with the Malay community. Planting padi is seen as the planting of wisdom

Pandan = Leaves used in food production as it is fragrant

Cucumber = Used in diet to stay young

Onions = Treat internal body wounds

Turmeric = Treat internal body wounds

Basil = Food (soaked in hot water to make tea, can increase appetite), used in poetry when love is unrequited

Bonus - Peranakan Penang Poetry!

As a reward for persevering, here is more poetry only this time from Penang!

The Peranakans mainly settled in the Straits Settlements of Malacca, Singapore and Penang. Then in the early 20th century, Penang was overrun by refugees from China. This was when the Peranakans in Penang started speaking Hokkien rather than Baba Malay.

The following poems are taken from:

A TAPESTRY OF BABA POETRY by Johny Chee.

According to Dato' Wong Kam Hoong "Penang Baba or Peranakan Hokkien is exceptionally unique. The dialect is basically a blend of the Hokkien dialect with Malay and English, interspersed with a sprinkling of words from other languages and Chinese dialects. Not only is there an assimilation of a substantially high number of Malay words into the Penang Baba Hokkien, the soft-spoken, melodious inflection of the spoken dialect is also much akin to that of the Malay language. This makes Penang Hokkien very pleasing to the ears of non-speakers."

Mother

Lu siu kho chi wa khi,
Cia u tong kim ei jit ci,
Bou lun hong, bou lun ho,
Ka wa cin sim lai ko

O what you went through for my upbringing
So that I'd become what I am today,
Regardless whether it's stormy or raining
You really showed love and care every day.

Familiar ditties:

1   A-B-C, tua pui ee cu kali

     A-B-C, fat aunty cooks curry

2   Chiou ka bueik lau jiou

     Laugh laugh laugh all you can
     Laugh until you've wet your pants.

3   Bou lui bo, kam ciak kho
     U lui bo, sinag ka ho

     A poor wife could withstand suffering
     But a rich one would be domineering.

Some 4-line rhymes

1.   A pek khi chui ta,
    A pou khi lata,
    A pek souk aphien,
    A pou khua liau gien

    Grandpa's thirst unslaked,
    Grandma's in a fit,
    Grandpa opium takes,
    Grandma craves for it.

2.   Ang Ka bo,
    Phak lou ko,
    Cei Lang chia,
    Chuei a co.

    The husband and his bride,
    Are beating the drums merrily,
    Then both go for a trishaw ride,
    To pay a visit to old granny.

More Ditties

This next section of ditties is taken from Raymond Kwok's
HOKKIEN RHYMES AND DITTIES

Ah Phien (Opium)

Ah Phien Sneh Ti Thor,
Choo Liau Kor Kor,
Bo Chiak Teong Hor,
Chiak Liau Hor Thor,

Opium comes from the earth,
Cooking makes it sticky,
Don't take it and all is well,
Eat it and you will become reckless,

Bor Knia Im Khor,
Chin Chnia Thnui Lor,

Neglecting wife and children,
Relatives will sever all ties with you,

Heng Kham Chnia Lau Thui,

Your ribs will resemble a flight of stairs,

Patt Thor Tnua Chui Kui
Khar Thooi Tnua Chau Mek,
Wa Piak Cheng Khor.

Your tummy a water-barrel,
Your legs like a Grasshopper's
And you will have to lean against the wall to put on your trousers.

Some 4-line rhymes

1. **Chih Knia**

   Chih Knia, Bo Kar
   Siang Kha Chih Goo,
   Chih Chow-Wa Bo Kar
   Siang Kar Chih Too!

   Raising a son without educating him
   Is like rearing a cow.
   Raising a daughter without educating her,
   Is like rearing a pig!

Notes: Timely advice on the importance of education. I like how they believed not just in the education of the sons but also the daughters.

2. **Chiak Pah Khoon**

   Chiak pah Khoon,
   Tan jee oon,
   Khoon pah chiak,
   Tan hoe giak!

   After eating, sleep.
   Waiting for fate.
   After sleeping, eat,
   Waiting to be rich!

Notes: Description of someone who hopes to get rich without working.

K.P.C.

K.P.C.
Keh Po Chee!
Sampat Ee
Bo Lang Chnia,
Ka Kee Th'nee

K.P.C.
Busybody!
Ignorant Aunty.
Nobody invites.
Takes Another Helping!

Notes: An uninvited guest and the ire they incur.

Leng Kau Leng

Leng Kau Leng
Hong Kau Hong
Ung-ku Kau Tom-Mong!

Dragon associates with Dragon
Phoenix mixes with Phoenix
The Hunch-back mixes with the coconut kernel

Notes: Ditty reflecting class consciousness of the Peranakans.

Raymond Kwok compiled:

HOKKIEN RHYMES & DITTIES: DOWN MEMORY LANE

to help preserve the form, clarity and uniqueness of Peranakan Penang Poetry.

My selection process

It was hard.

I mainly tried to select what I hoped others would like but also any that I thought informative or that appealed. Some bits of ditties were familiar but unfortunately, I couldn't find any ditty/poem which was 100% familiar. I hope that the sample of poems that I selected from Raymond Kwok's and Johny Chee's books will make others want to read them all.

I hope that mainstream bookshops will start carrying these books. And that soon the young will re-start the process of writing poems for their generation and enjoyment.

Kam siah!

Theresa
20th of September 2025

My panton

The Author as a little girl
(Here I am at the bottom of the driveway of the family home. How I wish I could once again turn around, walk up the driveway, and enter that front door.)

    Koh Chee, Kong Kong, Ng Ko, Mama,
    Rumah kosong. Lu pi mana?
    Tapi dengar Chakapan Baba,
    Mungka semua depan mata.

Translation:

    Koh Chee, Kong Kong, Ng Ko, Mama,
    Empty house. Where have you all gone?
    But when I hear Baba Malay,
    Faces all before me appear.

Explanation

My grandfather used to play the violin. I just assumed that it was something that was common but while researching this book, I discovered that if an instrument was mentioned that it was often the violin so I assume the violin was a popular instrument among the Peranakans.

I know that it was my grandfather's love of music and performing that led to him meeting my grandmother.

This poem was the last piece of homework that my teacher had us do. I am so glad that I did it. Just as I am so glad that I have gone on this journey to learn panton. Thank you for coming with me.

I hope you have enjoyed it.

Glossary

Chakapan Baba = The language of the Peranakans
Dengar = Hear
Depan = Front
Koh Chee = Father's younger sister
Kong Kong = Grandfather (My father used to spell it kun kun)
Kosong = Empty
Lu = You
Ng Ko = Father's younger brother
Mama = Grandmother
Mana = Where
Mata = Eye
Mungka = Face
Pi = Go
Rumah = House
Semua = All
Tapi = But

Dedication

Koh Chee and me

This book is dedicated to the late Eunice Kee nee Chan, my Koh Chee, who was like a second mother to me. Here we are in the front garden of the family house.

I love you so very much, Koh Chee!

NOTES

Baba Malay or Chakapan Baba or the Baba language was born when Chinese traders sailed down to Southeast Asia and intermarried with the local women. A mix of Hokkien and Malay, Baba Malay went into decline after WWII as many Peranakans were killed.

This is one of the reasons why there are no Baba Malay equivalent to some words today. When in doubt English words are often used.

Another reason for the decline is language integration.

Baba Malay has two registers:

1. Alus i.e., a refined form that women tended to speak
2. Kasair i.e., a coarser version practised by men.

Baba Malay tended to be spoken rather than written so there are many variations in the spelling e.g.,

kreja or kerja (work)

When in doubt I referred to Kenneth Chan's *Baba Malay For Everyone - A comprehensive guide to the Peranakan language* as well as William Gwee Thian Hock's *A Baba Malay Dictionary.*

Baba Malay is also sadly considered an endangered language.

Let's do our best to change this!

Bibek Theresa

About the Author

Theresa Fuller

Theresa Fuller has always loved stories and story-telling, but it was not until the birth of her first son that she became a full-time writer. Her aim was to write stories about her culture: Southeast Asia.

Theresa was Head of Computing at various private schools in Sydney. She has also been a Higher School Certificate (HSC) Examiner and HSC Assessor. Her teaching degrees have seen her work in primary and secondary schools and at Kalgoorlie College in Western Australia.

Her first published novel in 2018 was *THE GHOST ENGINE*, a steampunk fantasy about the fictitious granddaughter of Ada Lovelace, the world's first programmer. Theresa has published two books on Southeast Asian mythology: *THE GIRL WHO BECAME A GODDESS* (2019) and *THE GIRL SUDAN PAINTED LIKE A GOLD RING* (2022).

In 2023, *WHERE CRANES WEAVE AND BAMBOO SINGS* a visual narrative textbook for children and beginner writers was published.

In 2024 - *EATING THE LIVER OF THE EARTH* - collection of the lost folktales of the mousedeer Sang Kanchel was published.

In 2020, Theresa lost many family members. She threw heself into researching her family history as a way to deal with her grief. This was when she discovered that the language of her ancestors - Baba Malay - was on the verge of extinction. As a writer, teacher and selfpublishing author, Theresa found herself in an unusual position - she was able to create the curriculum that was needed to help fill a vacuum.

The result is the **Baba Malay Today** series.

All in aid of saving the language.

www.theresafuller.com

Thank you for your support!

More Books in the Baba Malay Today Series

Book 1 - Interrogatory Part I   SAPA, APA, MANA *or*
WHO, WHAT, WHERE

Book 2 - Interrogatory Part II   AMCHAM, APASAIR, BILA *or*
HOW, WHY, WHEN

Book 3 - Conjunctions   TAPI, ABIS, PASAIR *or*
BUT, SO, BECAUSE

Book 4 - Prepositions   ATAIR, KAT, BAWAH *or*
TOP, NEAR, BOTTOM

Book 5 - Antonyms   ALUS, KA, KASAR *or*
DELICATE, OR, COARSE

Book 6 - Essence   CHAKAPAN BABA ATI *or*
THE HEART OF BABA MALAY

Book 7 - Poetry   CHAKAPAN BABA PANTUN *or*
THE POETRY OF BABA MALAY

Book 8 - Idioms   CHAKAPAN BABA CHAKAPAN *or*
BABA MALAY IDIOMS

Note: In Standard Malay, the word 'hati' means the liver/heart i.e., the core. The word 'ati' in Baba Malay actually means 'liver'. Heart is 'jantong'. But phrases such as 'kind-hearted' and 'evil hearted' in Baba Malay are 'ati baik' and 'ati pekong' respectively. Not 'jantong baik.' Hence, I have used 'ati' to express the meaning of the word 'essence' or the core.'

    In Standard Malay, peribahasa is generally used to mean idiom, proverbs etc. However, in William Gwee's: a baba malay dictionary, on page 53, we find "chakapan what is said; a saying (e.g. an idiom)". Hence, I have used chakapan to mean idiom.

Dear Reader,

Thank you for the purchase of this book.

Please help us spread the word as we try to save our language.

If you wish to learn more, here are some books:

A Baba Malay Dictionary by William Gwee
A Grammar of Modern Baba Malay by Nala H. Lee
Ala Sayang by Felix Chia
A Tapestry of Baba Poetry by Johnny Chee
Baba Malay for Everyone by Kenneth Y.K. Chan with Amelyn Thompson
Chinese Peranakan Heritage in Malaysia and Singapore by Tan Chee-Beng
Hokkien Rhymes and Ditties down memory lane by Raymond Kwok
Malay Echoes from The Past - Penang Hokkien, Baba Language by Raymond Kwok
Pantun Pilihan Peranakan Baba Negeri Selat, 1910-1930-an Editor Ding Choo Ming
Penang Hokkien-English Dictionary with an English-Penang Hokkien Glossary
  by Tan Siew Imm
The Babas by Felix Chia

In 2024, I published a new series - New Peranakan Tales. These are bilingual and blended readers.

Let's all work together to save our heritage.

Bibek Theresa

Sydney, 25 of March, 2024

Coming Soon!

Books in the New Peranakan Tales Series

Gua Pi Keday	I Went to the Shops
Satu Taon Jalan-jalan	A Year of Walks
Binatang	Animals

Want to know when my next book will be out?

Go to www.theresafuller.com

Join my newsletter!

And never miss out again.

Other books by the author

The Ghost Engine

The Girl who became a Goddess

The Girl Sudan Painted like a Gold Ring

The Girls Who became Islands (Coming 2026)

Where Cranes Weave and Bamboo Sings

Eating the Liver of the Earth

www.theresafuller.com

Thank you for your support!

Presentations

I have been giving presentations on my research since 2023. If you are interested, please join my newsletter. I have spoken at the Peranakan Association of NSW, Burwood Language Festival, Australian Fairy Tales Conferences, Sydney Language Festival, Peranakan Sayang Festival, and the Polyglot Gathering.

Recently, I have started online presentations.

Want to know when my next presentation will be?

Go to www.theresafuller.com

Join my newsletter!

Places are limited so sign up quick!

www.ingramcontent.com/pod-product-compliance
Lightning Source LLC
Chambersburg PA
CBHW061217070526
44584CB00029B/3875